From the Psalms to the Cloud

From the Psalms
TO THE CLOUD
Connecting to the Digital Age

MARIA MANKIN & MAREN C. TIRABASSI

THE PILGRIM PRESS
CLEVELAND

The Pilgrim Press, 700 Prospect Avenue, Cleveland, Ohio 44115,
thepilgrimpress.com
© 2013 by Maria Mankin and Maren C. Tirabassi

Scripture quotations, unless otherwise noted, are from the New Revised Standard
Version of the Bible, © 1989 by the Division of Christian Education of the National
Council of Churches of Christ in the United States of America, and are used by
permission. Changes have been made for inclusivity.

Printed in the United States of America on acid-free paper

17   16   15   14   13   5   4   3   2   1

Library of Congress Cataloging-in-Publication Data

Mankin, Maria I.T., 1983–
     From the Psalms to the cloud : connecting to the digital age / Maria I.T.
   Mankin and Maren C. Tirabassi.
        pages cm
   Includes index.
   ISBN 978-0-8298-1932-8 (alk. paper)
     1. Communication—Religious aspects—Christianity.   2. Social media.
   3. Online social networks—Religious aspects—Christianity.   4. Prayer—
   Christianity.   I. Title.
   BV4597.53.C64M36 2013
   261.5′2—dc23   2013033250

DEDICATION

• • •

to Kim Martin Sadler,
whose spirit lights so many pages

• • •

Contents

• • •

INTRODUCTION

Into the silence cloaking me around,
Into the overarching solitude,
The stillness of this early morning hour,
I step with quiet confidence and trust.
I bring myself, my thoughts, my fears, my hopes,
The rushing, tumbling chaos of my mind,
The burdens of a busy yesterday,
The pressing choices that await today,
I sit, I wait; I yearn to hear you speak
Out of the silence cloaking me around.

—Isobel de Gruchy

WE HAVE WRITTEN LONGER BOOKS MORE QUICKLY. WE HAVE WRITTEN books about profoundly serious issues with more facility. We have edited contributors in greater numbers with global partners from many different time zones and with youth who, in their own way, could be said to live in different "time zones," too.

From the Psalms to the Cloud has been different. It has been a more reflective process, a deeper one. This is counterintuitive because reflecting on care for prayer life in a digital age seems to demand the same urgency our instantaneous communication encourages. Isn't technology just a speedy delivery system? Isn't the cultural buzz all about the shiniest way to put information instantly in reach of the seeker? Yes, but also no.

The original seed of an idea for this book grew out of our discussions about the critical challenges churches face in reaching faith seekers wherever they are, whether it be in the pews, out in the world, or behind a computer screen. We found ourselves pushing back against our own presumptions about what the church needs, and what we need, and what followers of all ages, abilities, and backgrounds may want. We have questioned how the spirit reaches all of us. In some moments, we have been on fire with the possibilities of ever-changing technology; in others, we were desperate for a quieter, more peaceful approach to God's presence within. We started this book imagining we knew where to get answers. Many answers were uncovered, but we also ended up with new questions.

So it is with a living faith. We cannot stand still, even for that moment at the center of a labyrinth, or in the midst of a nonviolent Twitter revolution, or when receiving a prayer e-mailed halfway around the world and written line by careful line by a youth group. We cannot stand still because people are lonely and needy and passionate, both behind their screens and in person. We cannot stand still because the desire for connection has not faded even if the methods for reaching out have changed. We cannot stand still because people need the church to keep moving forward. We can, however, rest. We can meditate. We can write and rewrite our songs of praise and our prayers of lament. We can give ourselves space to understand that it is the delivery system that has changed, not the faith itself. Not our love for each other, or our anguish, despair, celebration, frustration, confusion—these things remain the same.

A living church should constantly and humbly seek to learn new ways to reach and touch and care for people. Some people say that the changes in this digital age are as radical as at the time of the Gutenberg Bible. We should look even further. The call to tell God's good news through every new "app" or "link" has been happening since Pentecost—that first delivery system shake-up from comfortable scrolls to speaking in tongues. It is a part of the complicated burden and joy of our active faith. In the following pages, we try not to get hung up on offering specifics about technology, which change each day, but rather suggest that faith communities download the Great Commission in every new way possible, seeking the advice and gifts of the unexpected and often quite young evangelists and seekers when the old ways need a refresh.

In exploring these ideas for *From the Psalms to the Cloud*, we gathered many different voices from the United States, Aotearoa (New Zealand), Argentina, Canada—and, within Canada, a First Nations contributor—the Czech Republic, England, South Africa, and Zimbabwe. We invited everyone into an intentional spiritual practice, which we describe in the first chapter, and then together, and separately, we wrote prayers.

We were moved by what we received, personally and deeply. It was more than being moved; we were also settled, quieted, grounded. We invite readers of this book to be engaged in an intentional, spiritually informed writing of prayers for the people of this digital age, whether they are in the pews of our churches each Sunday, wander in once to a worship service, or attend a single event held at the church. Others pass through to attend a recovery group, shop at a food pantry, pick up a preschooler, or simply follow a sermon blog without so much as a "like" to betray their presence.

Readers have permission to use and adapt freely the resources we have provided for personal and congregational use. Please feel free to reprint the prayers and liturgy as well in the context of a faith community. Credit each writer and the book when you do so.

It's been an honor for us to be entrusted with these faith-full words. Putting them together to share with the wider community has been a transforming experience. Our thanks go out to every contributor, and to all of those people who helped and encouraged the participation of family members, friends, parishioners, students, and teachers around the world. You know who you are—you sharers, re-posters, re-bloggers and pick-up-the-phone folks. Thanks as well to Kim Martin Sadler, our editor with The Pilgrim Press, who has long guided us, inspired our work, and encouraged passionate grace in our words. We appreciate the work of Kristin Firth and Rick Porter for the copyediting and layout—it is no easy task to take the complications of worship formatting and make a book beautiful! Katie Fiegenbaum, our sensitive translator from the Spanish, makes herself available day and night. We are, also, as always, grateful to our incredible and supportive families and friends: in particular, we thank David Mankin and Donald Tirabassi, for their spirit-igniting conversations, patience, and love.

We are a body made up of many parts, and, if the writing of this book has shown us one thing more deeply, it is that if one part suffers, every part suffers with it; if one part is honored, every part rejoices with it. In these pages, we suffer and rejoice together, and in the holy word we say together, amen.

1

FAQS OF THE APOSTLES

Opening the Connection

DEAR PRAYER TEAM—FIRST, MY APOLOGIES. I WAS CLEANING OUT the diaper bag and found slips of prayers from this past Sunday tucked in among the toys and snack wrappers. Not where they should have been this week . . . they should have been in your hearts and minds. So sorry. But I suppose prayer is always a bit messy isn't it? And always tucked in among the riff-raff of the everyday? Will you pray on these prayers from our community? Thank you. Ellen

These words came as a scrap to us as well. They are not, after all, a prayer contribution, nor could we say that Ellen O'Donnell was sharing her spiritual practice as she prepares for intercession, though often the spiritual practice of prayer involves losing before finding. In fact, these words came from one of us to the other with this highlighted tag—"not sure where to put this."

Right at the beginning of the book.

This book is a conversation, not a cookbook. It looks a little like a worship anthology and we have both been associated with worship anthologies in the past. Certainly there are prayers here. Fortunately, we never called them "submissions," because once we started to receive, curate, care for these prayers—not second-hand clippings from some favorite worship service, but gifts for those who will read this book—we discovered they are the most feisty of written words. Cool down, flash fiction; be still, anime; grow humble, you polemics of political pundits—prayer is here. Beautiful, bold, claiming a blessing for beloved people and . . . yes, messy and mixed up with the wrappers and the diapers and the everyday.

This book is a conversation about the writing of prayer. Those who accepted the invitation are as much represented by their reflections about their own spiritual practices and preparation for the writing of intercession as they are by the prayers and worship they created. The sharing of these experiences, of creating space for prayer, as well as "samples" of prayers that have been so lovingly written and sent out into the world, extends the invitation for an intentional practice of prayer-writing to others. Sharon Benton is a pastor in Colorado. She wrote this:

> Perhaps I was a scribe in a previous life, because I write and re-copy. And edit and re-copy. All on lined paper in a spiral-bound hardcover notebook. With a Sharpie pen. In green. Or pink. Or whatever color shines for me in that prayerful moment. I begin writing my prayers in the early morning, coffee in hand and a cat in my lap. The snippet of a song lyric from my alarm clock may lead me to a subject, or a lingering conversation nudges me to put words on the page—randomly. I write to ask God what's needed—for the situation—for me. Eventually I notice what image of God is most present in that moment: Rock and Refuge, Divine, Holy One. If a scripture passage resonates with the experience, I sift through its impressions: eagles' wings, Spirit, perspective, breathless, weary, etc. I write stream-of-consciousness letter-prayers to God. I ask inappropriate, snarky questions or whine or beg—and eventually I come to the prayer. And then I re-copy. Part of my practice is pen-on-paper repetition. Letters to God. Letters bringing a situation or person to God's attention (and my own) over and over again.

When we invited people to write, pen to paper, or fingers to keys, we encouraged them to use the more structured short form often associated with social sites like Facebook or Twitter. This connected well with how people feel comfortable communicating these days. Turning often shallow interactions into a time of prayer and reflection was more powerful than we could have imagined.

The likelihood of someone (especially if that someone is not a minister) calling a friend and praying with them on the phone is slim these days. The ability to text or send a prayer electronically, however, is easy and familiar, an untapped resource for sharing our gratitude, fear, healing, and love. The difference between the reflective personal prayers like those we have gathered here and the drab ubiquitous forwarding of online photos of flowers and shallow sentiments can be life-changing, and not just for the person on the receiving end.

Hospital pages of caring and independent networking sites like Facebook can provide a space for medical updates and shared prayer. The heartfelt words on an online obituary create a forum for encouragement and comfort far beyond what we might have imagined a few years ago. During natural disasters, we have seen how quickly the right message calling for help on Twitter can motivate a whole nation of people to extend not just sympathy but donations as well; likewise, it's not uncommon for a person to send out a message imploring kind words, and prayers, on behalf of a loved one who has unexpectedly lost a job. These geographically scattered but electronically cohesive pray-ers might never set foot in a hospital room, attend visiting hours in a funeral home, or see some destruction firsthand, yet the tangible, typed sharing of compassion may very well be returned to again and again when needed, perhaps in the middle of the night, a year or two after the original occasion.

Who are these people, these strangers—these good Samaritans—who pause to lend a word, however they are able, from wherever they may be? In Christian faith, where we respect a Teacher who chose metaphors and parables over philosophical premises, we must pay attention to the parables of digital exchange—a link is a business connection, a friend a personal one, a post our Emily-Dickinson-letter-to-the world, a pin an idea to return to, a flicker the way in which one person sees beauty in what hundreds pass by as ordinary, and a tweet . . . well, it reminds us that God's eye is on the sparrow, knowing the tiniest rising of wings and the desperate falling to the ground.

Sue Donnelly reflected on her own online prayer practice that involved a long-term commitment when a close friend was in need:

When a dear friend of mine was going through a long hard year of chemotherapy I prayed for her every morning and shared the prayer in a short e-mail. I thought about what she may have been facing that day and asked God to hold her through it all. The writing seemed a way to pray continuously—words put down are out there—repeating and repeating. I learned that this kind of habitual, repetitive prayer builds connections with God. The practice helped me expand my awareness of the invisible struggles many are facing each day. While my written prayer focused initially on my friend, throughout the day it expanded in and out of me as a blessing for everyone I encountered. That acute awareness that everyone is battling something has not left me.

The movement of empathy and spirit from the friend to a stranger is very powerful. Note how Sue's practice is repetitive, intentional, written, shared, and universalized. It is no less a connection with God because of any of these elements.

Prayer writing also can move in the other direction—from a stranger observed to a deeper understanding of the friend. Molly Baskette shared with us this recollection about another one of our contributors, her friend and parishioner Kathleen Moore, who passed away a few months before this book was completed:

Kathy died so beautifully, and she had just become a Christian maybe three years ago. She was a lifelong radical feminist who thought organized religion was for idiots, mostly. Then she came to us "for community" she said, apologizing that she didn't believe more. Then she got cancer. And was so clear-eyed and calm about dying! She taught all of us a lot. . . .

When we heard about her death, we were moved to look back at the last e-mail Kathleen had sent to us and were stunned by how clearly Molly had articulated this woman's patient and beautiful faith. As Kathleen herself told us:

Maybe this is something I need to tell myself: to stop trying to be glib, witty, entertaining. It would be a great spiritual exercise (too bad Lent is over) for me to spend a day saying nothing that doesn't truly need saying. I just have to think of the right environment, since I no longer work and don't want to be rude to visitors. Maybe that next Bible discussion group I might attend. I've had bosses criticize me for not being glib enough, quick enough to offer a simple answer when I don't think there is one, so I know there's some pressure out there to be a know-it-all.

Wouldn't we all be a little better off, though, if we did carry a little of Lent around with us all year along? And a little of Easter, too, for the joy of it? Maybe even Christmas, to recapture our sense of wonder and earthy incarnation? What could we say to each other, to ourselves, if we unabashedly carried our faith around in our hearts, regardless of the season? What would we say and what would we delete? Would we discover how few words are really needed to share the best parts of ourselves? If we stopped speaking and posting and tweeting every single thought we had, and instead paused, considered, rested, would we discover that we have the capacity for a much deeper and maybe even simpler faith? Those few words would be more than verbal or digital ephemera—they would be contemporary psalm.

Later in this conversation, we will share some of the ways in which we invited our fellow pray-ers to prepare themselves so that when they came to the city park, the bistro, the train, or the dinner table, they were thinking about the drama behind the masks of other journeyers rather than checking a twitter feed for updates of someone else's shopping trip, or worrying about the future agenda for the evening's committee meeting, or rehearsing the past by imagining what clever response might have been delivered in a crabby breakfast exchange.

From the Psalms to the Cloud celebrates the possibilities of personal and spiritual connection that have come from social media, and the brevity in language that is its gift to the contemporary style in writing—what might be called the return-to-haiku blessing of it. We are also listening with the respect that is imitation to Paul the Apostle's wisdom when he was in Athens and preached on the Areopagus, not using his traditions or insisting on a Jerusalem path to understanding Jesus, but quoting the Phaenomena of Aratus and attending to the landscape of stones around him, including the altar to the unknown god and the longing it expressed. Paul's legacy includes ongoing borrowings like rosary beads, stained glass in an era when reading skills were limited, beer tunes, and Christmas trees. Why not Twitter, Google+, YouTube, Skype, and the next new sweet twist of code? We need to take social media into account if we wish to connect with not one but many different generations who use it.

There is another side to social media, of course. Every form of technology, and especially those we use to communicate, has its challenges. As a church, we need to be inside of the community of practice so that we can respond to those deep dysfunctions—the distractibility, personal isolation, and Internet addictions. If we don't understand this landscape, if we don't find a way to fold our best sense of self into meeting others where they are comfortable—and for many, this will not be in the pews, but online—how will we be able to relate to the challenges, the loneliness, and the sense of misunderstanding that bubbles up when communication becomes crisis? We must stretch ourselves, make a place for ourselves in the world we live in, and as we do that, we must also accept that the world today will not be the same tomorrow. Cody Maynus said it well: "I don't know what ministry will look like in the next year, ten years, fifty years. I think that social media gives faith communities the unique opportunity to respond to a deep spiritual hunger that is not being satisfied by the traditional parish structure." Just as we do in our faith, we must be ready to respond and to adjust to the changes that come. It isn't easy, but then, neither is faith, or patience, or prayer.

If there is so much prayer "in the cloud," we may ask what the role of the church is in this ascension era. Are we supposed to just stare "cloud"-ward into heaven? Of course not. *From the Psalms to the Cloud* is about prayer. Church is experienced in such an amazing number of ways: worship, mission and faith formation, meditation and community, even eating together in the sacrament of Holy Communion and the sacrament of pot luck supper or pizza night in the youth group. The specific aspect that is worship, of course, contains many experiences. There is music, scripture, and sermon, the invitation to give and to receive, the embodiment of hands clasped in peace or laid on the heads or shoulders of others—all of these are essential elements. The most powerful, both in and out of the pew, however, is prayer.

In one of its incarnations, prayer is a subset of worship, which is a subset of church. While worship and the church cannot survive without prayer, prayer can flourish in the world on its own. It is much bigger than the structure we try to give it. Prayer happens in a variety of times and places. It is personal and communal. It is communication with God that travels in both directions—sharing and listening.

Church is often the place people learn to pray. Prayer does not necessarily come naturally; it is learned and nurtured. Liturgical prayer becomes a way people struggle into prayer personally. The little scraps of invocation, confession, or dedication—for better or worse—become the models for prayer. Historians are clear that many of the psalms were templates for prayer, not prayed as they were perfectly crafted, but prayed with new personal "joys and concerns" gently inserted into their lines.

In each chapter of this book, we examine a different aspect of this faith journey in a strange new world, experiencing them not as divergence, but as the same open cup offered to give shape to the well water of our prayers. Some of our contributors have grown up with this technology at their fingertips; others are still struggling to understand it. All of us, regardless of age, experience, title, or education, have paused to consider the challenges of fostering prayerfulness in the technological arena where we find ourselves living. This is not a simple task. It's a conscious decision to examine well-established prayer practices, and experience new ones, to test out new tools and new words, and to recognize that this opportunity is not a distraction from the pews or a replacement for the work or ministries we continue to do, but rather, essential growth—as individuals and within our churches.

In the next chapter, "Psalms to Twitter," there are prayers of intercession written by gifted writers from the United States and around the globe. We asked our contributors to consider several factors as they prepared and prayed. As a first step, we wanted to hear how people prayed, how they might write those prayers, and how they might want someone to pray for them. The second step, and the part with which many people, including us, struggled, was keeping the prayers succinct. We asked every writer to consider short forms of writing—everything from traditional collects, haiku or psalms, to texts and tweets. Human attention spans have diminished, and that was certainly in the minds of those who reflected. We asked people what they could say in 140 characters, and, although the end result skewed far from that goal, the guidelines still provoked reflection from the pray-ers. In struggling to keep things brief, they found new paths to prayer, fresh ways to look at familiar issues, and powerful, untapped resources within themselves.

While our chapter on prayer is the longest, we also investigated the possibility of liturgy created by a similar process. We have divided these contributions into two chapters. The first, "Vintage Wine in Vintage Wineskins, Uncorked," will provide liturgy for weekly worship services that utilize bulletins (or PowerPoint presentations with congregational response) to assist clergy and lay leaders, as well as chaplains and organizers of ecumenical worship events. Being creative with "bulletin pieces" such as calls to worship and invocations, confessions and assurances of grace, offertory invitations and dedication prayers, litanies and benedictions takes time often absorbed by pastoral responsibilities. While these prayers can be used in services during those busy weeks, they are also shared as conversation with pastors and lay worship leaders and an invitation to creativity. This is a collection in a wide range of styles and includes resources connected to lectionary readings as well as many that are not.

Worship services that use contemporary music, interactive preaching, and fluid worship space need similar bridges—gathering words, brief prayers, calls to commitment, and words of sending forth. In paperless worship, the worship leaders voice these bridges, but without thoughtful preparation, the extemporaneous can become repetitive. "A Juice Bar in Cana" offers a variety of worship words for one and two voices and creative formats for call and response to engage the worshipers. They may be used directly by pastors and lay leaders, or as prompts. This chapter, and the preceding one, follow the order of the seasons of the church year, but we decided to start with September—the middle of the long Pentecost season. It seemed positively wicked, but Paul's speech to the Athenians was still echoing in our minds, and we wanted to recognize that it is the time many congregations begin their programming.

In "A Flash Mob of Angels," we share our own suggestions for revitalizing personal spiritual practice. Part of our hope in creating this book was that it might nurture both prayer-writers and faith communities, and, in order to do this, we realized we would have to go beyond the prayers and worship of others and provide a road map, or at least the suggestion of GPS, for the curious faith traveler. This is not an exhaustive list, but we do hope it offers a starting point for people looking to refresh their self-reflection. In addition, these exercises may be used in a group context as a way to create safe and inviting settings for the writing of prayer and liturgy. They may be useful for youth and young adult contexts, as well as small group ministries, church committees, mentoring of seminarians, and spiritual direction.

The final chapter, "In the Cloud of Faith" is a more formal conversation. We considered it crucial to discuss the relationship between the church and the wider world we interact with online. Why is it important for a church to be connected to the community through social media? How can the Internet facilitate faith connections, especially among audiences of widely varying different ages and abilities? How can a church avoid being caught in a technology that's no longer relevant to the audience? And as the technology evolves, what can churches do to continue to reach out to the younger members without alienating older members? We posed these questions to several of our contributors, and each of them sent back thoughtful, and very different, perspectives. It became clear to us that just as there are many voices longing to be heard so too are there many ways to go about doing that, as well as ideas about why it should be done.

One of the things we discovered while writing *From the Psalms to the Cloud* was that there exists a widespread and communal fascination with this subject. The struggle between faith and technology resonates with people from every part of the world, no matter the age or background. We all are working to find the balance between a healthy life and thriving faith, especially when faced with the constant barrage of distractions. It's difficult for many of us to imagine what it might be like if we took the time to reflect, pause, and quiet the spirit before we shared ourselves and our faith with the world beyond our keyboard.

There is great power in what we choose to say and to type, and with that comes great responsibility. We are stewards of the world, and it is a privilege, not a right, to be caretakers; we must pray, cherish, respect, and act only with our best intentions. We must adapt to the world as it is—not as we might wish it to be or remember that it once was—so that we may continue to share justice and tolerance, meet strangers only to realize that they may be friends, and discover the student waiting patiently within to guide us through the ever evolving maze of a complicated and compassionate faith.

2

FROM PSALMS TO TWITTER

Prayers of the People

To whom it may concern:
There was a moment today—
the first in years—
when I considered calling on you.
For an instant, it occurred to me
that you might not be
as I had decided you were.
I suddenly wondered if, instead,
you might be the one
whom I most need.
And my heart flash-flooded with hope.
If my suspicions are correct,
maybe we can start to talk again
as we once did.
Amen.

—*Vince Amlin*

Prayers. We pray. We write prayers. Often we do not know the One to whom we pray, and yet we do. Cody Maynus offers this reflection from his experience writing for this book. "As with most writing—secular or sacred, if that distinction even exists—I began with a blinking cursor. Midway through the writing of these prayers, I had the epiphany that, for me—a writer and a pray-er—God was in the cursor. . . . I lit a candle, as I always do when I'm writing (this time, the candle was a very excited orange pillar, about ten inches high and four inches in diameter). I then prayed, loosely and informally, for the Holy Spirit to move where She so desired. I then set to work praying and writing . . ."

PRAYERS OF NEED FOR NOW

Even as we learn more about lengthening our lives
we find new ways to kill and destroy.
Help us, O God, to find your peace.

Amid the chatter of e-mails and blogs and tweets,
lead us to the still places
where we can hear your voice, O God.

Faster, ever faster we move,
wanting newer and better and MORE.
Teach us that your love is always
simply enough for our needs.

—*Jerry Hebenstreit*

My hands are folded because she cannot fold her painful hands.
She is my sister. I am her shadow.
Together we pray for your touch, O Healing God.

—*LL Kroouze DuBreuil*

Sometimes our praying is a great boldness—as in these next words, a boldness of bridge-building.

If we believe in the healing and saving power
of God's love, who is both Father and Mother,
let us encourage each other to become bridge-builders
and declare ourselves the community
of God's plan that opens the way to all
who believe and trust in
restoring and liberating love.

Si creemos en el poder sanador y salvador
del amor de Dios, nuestro Padre y nuestra Madre,
animémonos a construir lazos entre las personas,
que afirmen que somos pueblo, que somos comunidad.
Y digamos, con claridad, que el plan de Dios
abre puertas a la salvación de todos y todas
quienes crean y confíen
en su amor restaurador y liberador.

—*Gerardo C. C. Oberman*

• • •

Prayer comes in all forms. It may flow as lightly as a poem, or sit, deeply ordinary —but nevertheless precious—in an e-mail inbox. Below is one such ordinary, precious letter from a year's worth that Sue Donnelly e-mailed to a friend struggling with cancer.

I pray you can inspire yourself with your own strength and wisdom and courage. And if your own source feels thin, consider all those hundreds of people who are holding you close in prayer and love and hope. This whipping is almost done. God lures through the long night and the morning alike. You will find it to be so again, and again and again and again.

—*Sue B. Donnelly*

Sharyl B. Peterson reflects that her practice is informed by tradition and scripture and experienced liturgically and therapeutically. "I sometimes use very familiar Psalms, like Psalm 23 and Psalm 100, as a basis for prayers. I've learned in nearly twenty years of pastoring that almost everyone is familiar enough with these Psalms and that using phrases from them can be very comforting for people":

Lord, you are our shepherd; and yet, right now there is much that _____ wants and needs.
We pray for your loving care and guidance for _____ this day, and in days to come.
Give _____ rest in green places
    that you, and beloved friends, prepare for them;
Lead them by still waters that will refresh them;
Strengthen and restore their souls.
Help them remember that you are with them in this journey,
    even in the deepest and darkest valleys.
Surround them with your goodness and mercy,
    that they may know they dwell safely with you and within you,
    now and always. Amen.

"Depending on how well I know the intended prayer-recipient, sometimes I will introduce an unfamiliar Psalm to someone in a particular prayer situation. It can be helpful for folks in need of prayer to discover that even the ancient ones understood and talked about some of the difficulties they are now facing. For example, Psalm 55 can be very helpful to people struggling with domestic violence, especially verses 12–14. My practice would be to read those verses of the Psalm to the care-receiver, reflect with that person on what she/he hears/experiences in the reading, then craft a prayer on the spot that lifts up his/her particular concerns":

It is not enemies who taunt me—I could bear that;
it is not adversaries who deal insolently with me—I could hide from them.
But it is you, my equal, my companion, my familiar friend, with whom I kept
pleasant company . . .

"Here is an approximation of a prayer crafted with and for a woman with whom I worked at one time, using this practice":

O God, we know that you know the pain (care-receiver name) is
   struggling with.
(Name of assailant)—her very best friend, the person she trusted most,
   has changed so much.
Her heart is breaking at his betrayal; she is frightened and hurting from
   his anger.
Help her trust, O Lord, in what you are whispering to her—
   that she is your beloved child,
   undeserving of this violence and pain.
Grant her strength of body, of mind, and of spirit,
   to name what is happening, and to deal with it helpfully and well.
Surround her with good and loving friends
   to encourage and support her in this hard time.
And please help (assailant) find his own healing as well. Amen.

—*Sharyl B. Peterson*

•◦◦•

"The practice that gave rise to this prayer started as something of a challenge," writes Kipp Gilmore-Clough, "to revisit, seriously, a scripture verse that carried the baggage of my unformed, relatively facile and hyperindividualized high school theology. Gradually, the verse shifted from a simplistic celebration of the self to a greater gratitude for the Source of that self and the processes in which it arose. I have not been made, but am still in the process of being made. And in that there is wonder, and cause for praise."

A PRAYER OF BECOMING

All around me, all within me is gift. You are ever on the move, ever calling forth, creative, playful, dazzlingly loving God. May I find joy within myself, wisdom in my flaws, amazement and gratitude in this ongoing process of becoming. I need not be that which I cannot be—self-sufficient, self-contained—because I am always a part of something far greater. O God, let this wonder sink in. Amen.

—*Kipp Gilmore-Clough*

• ❃ •

Cody Maynus was one of the writers who took the challenge to compose ultrabrief prayer most to heart. "Even though I knew there was a brevity limit, I wrote the prayers as I would for any ministry setting. Then, as with the Scriptures, I redacted. I cut. I added. I rethought. I spoke aloud. I tweeted and checked for character count. I took the prayer drafts to other folks—a Benedictine nun, my Lutheran pastor, my friend who is an atheist, my liturgy professor, and some of my peers—and asked for their commentary. The redaction continued. All of this occurred amidst the emotional and physical ravages of the weeks leading up to the end of term. At least one of the prayers became my personal prayer."

Short prayers such as these—redacted, rethought, shared—may be the psalms and collects of our digital age.

• ❃ •

First post or five thousandth,
DM, IM, tweet, text, or blog,
may my words reflect your Word,
Lover of my Soul!

—*Richard Bott*

• ❃ •

God of the smart phone and the smart heart, burn bright in me, longer then any LED battery.

—*Christy Ackley Zuzelo*

• ❃ •

God, sometimes I think the people I serve don't really want you close to them. When I feel this, I fail them. Show me I'm mistaken about them, would you please?

—*Alan F. Parker*

• •• •

I hope someday, God, I have done enough
that my kid thinks of me and tears up
when certain songs come on the radio.

—*Maria Mankin*

• •• •

TXTS OF ENCOURAGEMENT

1.
What in darkness
might seem lost
is a moment

in shadow
waiting for the light
to come

2.
if a seed dies it will rise
taking its time

don't be afraid of the dark
it is time of great growing

and you will see for yourself
just what you will become

—*Erice C. Fairbrother*

• ⚅ •

Kathleen Moore writes about the massive shift she felt when she took the time to really pay attention to the opportunity God offered—not just to pray for others, but also to feel herself changed because of the experience. "When I started with prayers for people, the first was for a specific person, a poet who sells his work on the street. I initially thought I'd buy a poem as an act of charity, and then was astonished at how good he was":

You who are The Word, bless Riccardo
With comfort and warmth.
Tell him, you who are The Word, that his words will live
In him and in others
In a place without fear, a stronghold of kind words and ample care.

—*Kathleen Moore*

• ⚅ •

Kipp Gilmore-Clough's reflection when he was praying using Psalm 139 also shines a light on Erice Fairbrother's prayer based in Psalm 121:

"I could see myself as percolating forth from the brewing of generations, more aware of my own cloud of witnesses, those people I knew in person and through story whose being I carry within my own. I am aware of their complicated humanity, which is reflected in my successes and in my failures, in those facets of myself that make me uncomfortable, and those that give me pleasure. Allowing for their flawed and glorious humanity allows for my own."

Prayers for others are not always intercession, but are also reflections on human connections—the obvious and not so obvious ones. Who are the flawed and glorious ones we carry into our psalms? You may wish to choose a psalm, consider your "cloud of witnesses," and link them together.

PSALM 121

When you are in the room
I am somehow stronger

When we are side by side
I am not so afraid

When walking and you talk to me
I know who I can be

And when I find myself alone I thank you
For being there

—*Erice C. Fairbrother*

• ◦◦ •

God, help us all to see with your lashless limitless eyes.
Have you misplaced all who have been shoved aside,
Too old, too young, too timid, too confident, too strange, too extra?
Did you find their worth in the work itself,
In the esteem and rewards of the work?
God, show these good people what you see in them.
Show it to us all.

—*Kathleen Moore*

• ◦◦ •

A COFFEE SHOP PRAYER

God, may time in this coffee house serve as sacrament: coffee and pastry and
a gathering around the table. The open invitation to receive hospitality is an
invitation to offer oneself into the mutuality of relationship and well-being.
You whose Being is ever poured out, help me to catch glimpses of you across
tables, overhear in the buzz the echoes of your grace. Amen.

—*Kipp Gilmore-Clough*

• ◦◦ •

Michele Jarmany surprised herself. She responds to our query about the process of praying with both a story and a prayer. "I do not have a set way of praying. Often I use passages from the Bible to reflect on. Sometimes I sit in silence and wait. But at other times experiences demand reflection and prayer.

"This is such an experience. I went to visit a young man and found I had pre-conceived ideas about what to expect. While I was listening to him I found to my surprise and shame that I was wrong. Christ tells us not to judge and if you have ears let them hear! I pondered that I had not been listening and that I had judged this person even before I had met him. This prayerful reflection was the result":

JOHN 17:20–23

I came with indifference
I thought I knew.

You are so different from me.

I listened
Expecting nothing.

I heard you

And then

I saw me in you!

I wasn't expecting it!

You are not like me at all
And yet I was there!

Me in you and you in me
Just like Christ said it could be.

Thank you God!

—*Michele Jarmany*

Sometimes the surprises are within oneself or in the landscape, natural and human, as in the following two prayers.

Does it matter, God,
if my faith has walls,
or if I walk alone?

I can love justice,
seek kindness, walk humbly,
God, all on my own.

What is this aching
though, God, this regret
when I always pray alone?

—*Maria Mankin*

•••

CHRIST TXTS FROM THE WILDERNESS

1.
the peace that was left
waits my eyes
wandering
over mountains catching it
calling

this peace
that's emerging
holding, sheltering
covering, bleeding
bending, birthing

the peace of our dreaming
the peace of the earth

2.
Would you like a drink?
I see you're on a journey
Take a moment
There is beauty here
Flowers
You might miss
Unless you stop—
Would you like to share
A cup with me?

3.
Welcome to the wild place;
The peace of the birds will sing to you
The leaves of the bush will caress you
The wind in the trees will move you

Here shadows will play with you
Light will restore you
Welcome to the heart
Of love's wilderness

—*Erice C. Fairbrother*

• ◌◌ •

Prayer is so often shaped by nature, by God's creation that is other than the human format of it. "Bush" (undeveloped land or country with native vegetation) in the first of these prayers is not a term unique to the southern hemisphere, but it is distinctive there. Often in Aotearoa, New Zealand, from which this prayer, a setting of Psalm 23, comes, "bush" is used to encompass an emotional and spiritual experience with nature.

BUSH PSALM

Loving God, you are the dear companion of my bush walks.
You lead me through a tall stillness of sun-splashed green, rinsed with birdsong.

How you satisfy my need!
The tracks you show me lead me ever deeper into awe and reverence for the
wonder of you.
When the way is steep and dangerous with mud and the climb seems
beyond my strength and courage, you are with me, enduring with me.
You sustain and enrich me with the discovery of so many wayside treasures.
In the shining of the leaves above me, you give me a patterned canopy
of blessing.
Like the deeply contented song of the fern-fringed creek, my soul sings in
gratitude for your abundance.
Surely the friendship of fantails, the peace of sunlit peat pools,
the tenderness of deep moss, and the purity of the bellbird's joy
are your abiding gifts to me.
I will dwell forever in the life giving green-ness of you.
Amen. So be it.

—Beverley L. Osborn

LAMENTING AWE

I gaze out beyond the mountain ledges in awe.
A child tugs restlessly on his mother's sleeve.
"Can we go now, I'm bored?"

The beauty of all that you have made,
The six-year-old child's inability to witness.
A cell phone rings, the child answers.
He is encompassed, turning from the view, from Your gifts
Already forgotten or never seen.

How do I rouse Your people to witness, O God?
To peel back the translucent synthetic curtain
We have draped across all you have made.

To listen for the music our human ears have been trained to block
The celestial trumpets, prophetic verse.
To hear and recognize, to take comfort in Your Word.
To empower these to step out, to follow, to serve—
Not the human mandate, but You.

—*Barbara Bruce Brakey*

• ◼ •

Conductor of the dawn,
who cues the first robin to the red berries in the holly bush today, send your
chorus of nest-builders to the Home Depot in my backyard for winter twigs
and dry stalks, bits of branch blown by storms, and decorative bright litter.

Allegro—their songs, my prayers, the ovation of the spring. Amen.

—*Maren Tirabassi*

• ◼ •

The prayers we share here are the boundaries, thin, very thin, between creation,
experienced in constellation, coneflower, corgi, and even gnats.

God who thunders, who boasts in glorious hills, who speaks in a
    still small voice,
teach us to clamor only in your praise, or in defense of the afflicted—
yet alert when a gentle word might move the afflicter.
Afflict us, not with hellfire but with biting gnats,
quick reminders to be still with our own praise,
our vain promises we will forget, our begging to be enough.
If biting gnats will not quiet us, speak loudly enough to tell us
    that we are enough,
need not augment ourselves with what we buy, what we boast.

Teach us to speak as you speak, in a resounding chorus of creation, with words so soft that we strain to hear.

—*Kathleen Moore*

• •

PSALM OF LONGING

It's hard to see the important thing
The simple thing
The central thing
The place that is pure
That is God in the heart
Where the mountain dances with colour

—*Erice C. Fairbrother*

• •

God, help me be like a leaf floating on this river of life; move me through the calm and turbulent times; don't let me sink.

—*Christy Ackley Zuzelo*

• •

PSALM FROM A RUNNER

I went for a run
Enjoying the sun
Where your pictures come
Barbed wire and beauty
Lovers side by side
With explorers
Speaking in languages
Yet to be born

—*Erice C. Fairbrother*

PSALM OF THE WAKATIPU

Almighty God, you were with me in my return to the Wakatipu.
You refreshed me with vision of mountains, peaks, and hills.
You touched me with the river that is the lake of the giant,
    with the blossoms and the birds of the air.
You thrilled me with jet planes and God-incidence.
You took me in safety through places where violence occurs.
You gave me helpful people and a secure lodging in which to rest.
Even when traffic was difficult and steps impossible,
You kept me in your care.
I felt no fear for I knew You with me, night and day.
You made it possible for me to be re-created
    by vision, by speech, by taste, by touch, and by insight.
I was nourished by your goodness and I know that You,
    Creator, Son and Spirit,
      are the Mystery in whose Energy, Life, and Love I survive.

—*A. Heather Kelly*

"I share this song, the result of a group effort in the context of Christian Worship Second Symposium, held at the Theological Community of Mexico, in collaboration with the Calvin Institute of Christian Worship and Red Crearte, Liturgical Music and Art Network," writes Gerardo Oberman. "We came up with this song as a group in ten minutes—then there was much polishing":

God, the seeds of your love's Realm
you call us today to sow;
in our daily lives on earth
in all times and every place.

(refrain)

They are in our hands,
not for us to keep.
God, the seeds of your love's Realm
you call us today to sow.

—*Gerardo C. C. Oberman*

• 🁢 •

BEACH PSALM

Living God, you are the best of friends for my beach walks.

You refresh me with the tang of salt and the music of gentle waves on calm days and brace me with gale gusts on days when the seas are a glory of crashing splendour.

You give me the smooth sand under my feet, coloured and patterned in satisfying swirls.

Even when I must clamber through jutting piles of driftwood or wend my way between sharp rocks, I'm not afraid because you are with me, giving me your adventurous spirit.

You provide me with wonderful vistas, ranging from glorious technicolour to the serenity of tender shades of mother-of-pearl.

When life gets overcrowded by the demands of others, when I'm berated for walking a beach instead of using the time in more "profitable" ways, you restore my perspective and renew my stamina.

Surely the wings of seabirds will weave panoplies of your light and blessing around me and the delicate structuring of small shells, scattered at my feet, will remind me that your care for me is individual and wonderful and is mine forever.

—*Beverley L. Osborn*

• 🁢 •

This is my home, this state
of the sage heavy air, the long hot runs, the jackrabbit crossings.
This is my home, and I love it
with all my heart and soul and mind.

But there are days, God, fitful hours
when I miss the shadowy northern pines, the sudden summer storms,
the family—crazy, infuriating, adored—
with all my heart and soul and mind.

This is my home, but there are days
when I stretch from coast to coast
with all my heart and soul and mind
and alone, God, alone, I am not enough.

—*Maria Mankin*

UNDER THE WEATHER

Cloud sitter, cirrus-silhouette,
who forecasts rays of light, gentle rain
and the rare rainbow
in the weather of sorrow,
find those lost in the cumulus of grief
or the fog of despairing,
remind them that ordinary sunshine
is conserved in every leaf,
in the skin of every human hand. Amen.

—*Maren Tirabassi*

REFLECTION FROM A HIKER

Your mountain looks so sheer
The footsteps you see
Are from companions
Who have climbed with us

—*Erice C. Fairbrother*

• ●● •

PRAYER FROM THE FOURTH COMMANDMENT

Mystery glimpsed in March blizzard
that breaks branches on old trees
dropping squirrel-homes to the level of beagle nose
and paints the Interstate with ice,
give me snow-wisdom—
to bring sled, not shovel, to my schedule,
snow-compassion—for homeless and home-bound—
and snow-play with wonderful fortresses
and the laying down of angels. Amen.

—*Maren Tirabassi*

• ●● •

Living the fourth commandment, the longest one, the one about Sabbath in any season, is very difficult in our time. Living simpler lives, slowing the pace, consuming less—these are significant issues for prayer for many. Sharyl Peterson speaks to this:

"I preach a fair amount on social justice, and on how our daily choices about eating, dressing, and making other consumer choices affect others with whom we share this world. Here are two brief prayers I wrote for folks considering/learning to compost, or to eat locally, or to make some other daily change in their lives that will affect our environment":

Lord, help us see the goodness around us,
    and to embrace it joyfully in our daily living. Amen.

God of bounty,
    help us learn that less stuff
    makes more space
    for us to live closer to You. Amen.

—*Sharyl B. Peterson*

• •• •

A PRAYER FOR SOMEBODY EMBRACING A SIMPLER LIFESTYLE

God: Help me get rid of the junk in my life—physical, emotional, spiritual—so I can be fully present to you, to my community, and to myself.

—*Cody E. Maynus*

• •• •

TASTE AND SEE THAT GOD IS GOOD, PSALM 34:8

God of feast and fast,
who relishes falafel, jambalaya, pad thai,
and counts points with the weightwatcher—
help us eat with compassion for the earth,
delight in many flavors, and
generosity in sharing.
Praise to you—
Locavore, Foodie, Eucharist! Amen.

—*Maren Tirabassi*

• •• •

We make it so hard to simply serve you, O God.
Teach me to want only what serves you,
to put aside whatever distracts from you.

—*Jerry Hebenstreit*

GLIMPSES OF SABBATH

The idea of carving time for rest from my massive to-do list oppresses me.
It's just impossible:
    one more item to check off,
    one more expectation to fulfill,
    one more possibility for failure.

God, you are busy. Yet you are free enough to rest.
I get glimpses of Sabbath. I think I want more.
Help me discover a holy moment—just one simple, undemanding, deep-
breath moment—
to enjoy some freedom.

—*Matthew Braddock*

Gracious and loving God,
We may not know it, but you do. . . . You know that we are good enough to
do this work. It isn't always clean. Just like the Jordan River where Jesus was
baptised. Just like John the Baptist, who thought he wasn't good enough.
When we don't feel good enough to be your servants or to pray or to pray
for others or to be prayed for, remind us God, that we aren't damaged goods.
That we ARE your Beloved. That through work, the work that Jesus does
through us, we are yours in all our humanness. Fill us with your spirit. Give
us the strength to let go of that feeling that we aren't good enough. Help us
be empathetic and do your work the best way we know how.

—*Christy Ackley Zuzelo*

Some of the prayers of intercession that were suggested emerged from the very real daily concerns of what has been called the "digital age." Kipp explores this idea during the naturally reflective space created by the season of Lent:

"During Lent, I tried a spending fast—refraining, as much as possible over the course of one week, from spending money. One observation that arose from this was that I have two types of spending rituals. One is relational—for instance, members of the choral group I sing with at church head to the local cafe together before worship each week. This is as much about enjoying the fresh air and catching up with each other as it is about the financial transaction in a cup of coffee. The other is more obsessive—a regular compiling and updating of lists of music to buy. What happens when I have gathered more than I can listen to? This becomes, then, a reflection of the ethos of living within consumer capitalism. Do habits of consumption mask neglect of something else, be it of the self or of the wider world?"

A CONSUMER'S PRAYER

Gracious God, if anyone knows about total expenditure, it is you—the giving forth of yourself to sustain this wild, tenuous, boundless creation of which we are a part. Heighten my mindfulness today of the ways in which I am intricately embedded within the economy of human relationship, the intertwined ecology of being. Bring to consciousness the means through which I expend my resources and myself. As I live and move, work and rest, think and play within your being, help me to remain unconsumed by my consumption, finding ways of spending and saving, both of which will increase my wholeness and bring blessing into the world. Amen.

—*Kipp Gilmore-Clough*

Dear God of abundant love,
Help us when we try to fill our emptiness at the shopping mall.
We know from experience, these efforts are futile.
We end up with walk-in closets, shoe racks, kitchen drawers,
    and bookshelves filled to overflowing.

At the end of the year we wonder why we have credit card bills that are high,
and college and retirement fund balances that are low.
Save us from our consumer-spending addictions.
Free us to sit with another living breathing human soul for an honest
conversation over a warm cup of tea.
Let it be so.

—*Cheri R. Holdridge*

God of the real world,
Lift my eyes from my screen, turn me away from the blue screen of death
and to the blue skies filled with life, with birds, with clouds.
Lift my hunched shoulders frantic over the keyboard and help me be like
the trees, tall, pushing up and out.

—*Christy Ackley Zuzelo*

Friday God,
who speaks through imams gathering the submitted,
flashes the foursquare in twenty-somethings' plans,
promises weekend to school child and office worker,
give us what we need in our time of needing—
the preaching, the party, or the pause—
so that we truly say, "TGIF"—
thank God it's Friday. Amen.

—*Maren Tirabassi*

Bless you, girl I knew then.
Float beyond that airy boundary of your own spirit;
Or perhaps it is time to march, to sprint even if your legs will not,
Somewhere outside, connected to more than you dare imagine.

—*Kathleen Moore*

• ▓ •

Vince Amlin names an inner spiritual circle in prayer writing that involves both the inspiration for prayer and the re-vision of prayer:

"I use a process that is more typical for me but that I also think is related to Revelation 21, 'write only what is trustworthy and true.' Each of my prayers began with an emotional spark, a strong image or feeling that came to me. I had no idea what shape these prayers would take, but I knew I had a prayer within me because of that spiritual spark. From there, I simply started writing what came to mind. Some of it was good, some not so good, and the way I could tell was to hold that spark up to each new line. The spark asks: 'Is this true? Is it clear? Does it belong? Or is it just writing, or ego, or distraction?' If the spark is strong, its light will last long after I've finished the prayer; and if the prayer is good, it will reignite that spark in me and in others."

From text to tweet, lead me only into the temptation to type truth.

—*Elizabeth D. Barnum*

• ▓ •

Holy One,
Forgive me for the times I said to my children, to my spouse, "just one second," as I write the random message to the random person to show how smart, witty, humorous I can be when my family, right there, knows all these things. God, help me show that I have nothing to prove to the Internet people of the world, that I have everything I need.

—*Christy Ackley Zuzelo*

• ◉◉ •

Oh God, to spend one less moment reading the comments
of ignorant bullies, or watching the minute movements of people
I barely know . . .

Worse even than the twenty-four-hour cycle
of violence in the news, this in-the-know
surface-scratching is an endless low-level disease
breaking down the body of faith. Where the one hand hates the other,
and the nose will do anything
to spite the face, we have abandoned deep and sacred breath
in favor of the shallower, unlearning regret of insta-retort.

Oh God, to hear your voice hushing
the rush of a million fingers typing—to sense that pause of exhalation
just long enough for you to imprint on my heart
how to begin to live into your grace
with a body less divided, a life less exposed—
for that moment of peace, God, I would be grateful.

—*Maria Mankin*

• ◉◉ •

I hold in my heart those who have hundreds of friends in cyberspace
    or on Facebook
But no one to walk with on the beach;
Those whose Internet social networks are vast
But have no one to hug them when they are down;
Those who have hours stretching out in front of them
And only a computer screen for company;
Those whose tweets, twitters, and FB messages are witty and clever
But who are afraid of closeness with a real human being.

May they be released from need and fear,
Freed to love and be loved.
May they be touched by grace and enfolded in peace,
Now and every day. Amen.

—*Lynne Frith*

• •• •

A FANGIRL'S PRAYER

You, criticized for your company
and your pursuit of fun,
you understand my unusual Sabbath.

You do not judge or hate or spew
against my fanning, or my enthusiasm,
at the friends I have made
who stretch around the world,
who give back my passion
seventy times seven.

You love as I do,
with all the fire of a thousand worlds.
You, loving and generous and silly and wild,
a God who understands the need for squee!

—*Anonymous*

• •• •

Oh, God.
It's 3 AM and I picked up my phone.
Again.
For the third time since going to bed.
Just one more glance at my status updates.
One more swipe through the tweets. One more . . .
Who am I kiddin'? It's not just one more.

It's a constant tap/flip so I can feel connected. Immersed. Virtualized.
Help me! Please?
To put down the phone.
To shut off the browser.
To focus here.
To be here.
To live here.
In this tangible now.
Oh, God! Help me . . . please?
. . .

It's 4 AM. I just picked up my phone . . .
Oh, God . . .
Amen.

—*Richard Bott*

•⚀•

Kind God, you call us to speak truth to a world riddled with untruths, to speak life to a world plagued by death. Fortify us by your Holy Spirit so that we can openly and honestly address the issues of Internet addiction—pornography, loneliness, excessive shopping—and speak life and truth to those who most need to hear it. Through Jesus the Christ, who liberates us from all bondage and sin. Amen.

—*Cody E. Maynus*

•⚀•

God, like You, the Internet remembers everything; it exposes our truths and our lies. And where there is one lie, there are often many more. Lord, I am drowning, well over my head trying to keep straight my fuzzy half-truths, my stories, trying so desperately to bottle up my feelings, to control my resentments, to control my own hurts, and to do damage control on the hurts I caused. I've lied to myself as much as I lied to You, to my friends, to my loved ones. Even when I felt like I hit rock bottom, I found a trap door.

Scared and in tremendous pain, beating myself up over and over, I wish for silence over the hard work of repairing my relationships, of repairing me. God, of grace, and compassion, remind me that we are ALL human and humans are beautifully imperfect and complex. Remind me that the beauty of rock bottom is that there is nowhere else to go but up, up through the deep waters to God's grace.

—*Christy Ackley Zuzelo*

• ▪▪ •

PRAYER FOR INTERNET DATING SITES

God, this is my quiet prayer of thanks
for the blessing of
(*Match.com* / *e-Harmony* / _____),
which connected me to the one I love.
You, who turn loneliness into companionship
in so many ways,
guided me to these still waters,
this anointing with oil,
and we are glad to dwell
in the house of your love forever. Amen.

—*Maren Tirabassi*

• ▪▪ •

PRAYER B4 POSTING, PHILIPPIANS 4:8

Whatever is untrue,
whatever is unkind,
whatever is unjust,
whatever is not love,
give me the strength, O God,
to delete.

—*Vince Amlin*

• ◘◘ •

Mary Beth Hartenstein credits the influence of other writers with enriching her prayer creativity. "I am so grateful to other writers, whose works I have used and read, who have helped to guide me to experiment with phrases and names and words. Reading their work has given me permission to try new things for myself as I dare to capture the essence of the moment in a prayer. It is my hope that through the words and images of the prayer offered, individuals connect with the Holy."

With these words on our hearts, we begin a short series of prayers about pregnancy, birth, infertility, adoption, fostering, the loss of pregnancy or a newborn child, and the choice to be a family that does not have children. Deeply significant to those who are in child-bearing years—and even to many who are not—these concerns invoke a very tender praying.

PRAYER FOR A PERSON/COUPLE EXPECTING THE BIRTH OF A CHILD

Creator, you birthed life from its beginning. There is new life waiting to be birthed now.

May this little one know goodness from the start. Allow joy to be a part of the beginning. Let love be the foundation of all that this little one will know. May nurture always be present. May hope always prevail. Protect now this little one until the day of his/her borning cry. Amen.

—*Mary Beth Hartenstein*

• ◘◘ •

FOR A PREGNANT WOMAN

I give thanks for your body
    and its silent intelligence
    carrying, holding, growing
    a new someone
    without ever reading a single pregnancy book.

I pray these blessings for this body:
    rest and good food;

and wonder and appreciation
for the giving of the gift this body will
     soon enough
bring into the light.

—*Amy Sens*

• •• •

God of already-mothers and those who long for the job,
You called the worlds into being with a word from your lips
You make it look so easy to create life
You never insinuated before how easily it could all go wrong
how tenuous it all is
Safeguard this velcro-baby in my womb
8 cells, 16 cells, 32,000
growing, clinging, sticking stronger every day
that along with Hannah, Elizabeth, billions of women ancient and modern
who longed to hold their own baby in their arms
I might trust
I might trust
I might trust
and let joy begin to outpace fear in the delicious adventure of pregnancy

—*Molly Phinney Baskette*

• •• •

PRAYER FOR THE PARENTS OF A STILLBORN BABY

Let us hold in our hearts _____ and _____ , whose long awaited
     daughter/son, _____ , died during/at birth.
Nothing can take away the loss of this precious life and the hopes that
     were dreamed for her/him.
May the love with which _____ and _____ are surrounded bring com-
     fort in their sorrow,

and each day bring healing of their grief and pain.

This is our prayer.

—*Lynne Frith*

• ⚄ •

God of already-mothers and those who long for the job,

Where were you, when those cells were knitting together in my womb?
Did you blink? Did you go out for a cigarette? Did you fall down on
the job, and is that why that little life fell out of me?

I longed to hold a baby in my arms in 8, 7, 6 months.

Instead, a dark screen where tiny pixels should have been blinking. Breath-
holding, fear filling my veins like dark water, silence from the lab tech.

Instead, I had to leave by the back door of the ultrasound lab so my sobs
wouldn't spook the happy pregnant women, ignorant of how close life
is to death.

Just to be clear: I long to hold a baby in my arms. Hear my cry! Help me to
heal, and trust You again!

—*Molly Phinney Baskette*

• ⚄ •

PRAYER FOR A PERSON/ COUPLE EXPERIENCING,
RECOVERING FROM TERMINATION OF A PREGNANCY

God, remind her that she is not alone. Remind her that she is not the only one.
Remind her that this termination, for her, was not only lamentation but also
liberation. Like so many, she has been shamed into harboring this decision as
secret. Bear loving witness to her testament to what would not and could not
be. Bear loving witness to this termination being a faithful decision. Bear loving
witness to her capacity for wisdom and wholeness, then, now, and always.

—*Elizabeth D. Barnum*

• ⚄ •

Up before dawn
we lay watching
the moon set

Our lives are so precariously
blessed I am afraid to take
on something, and someone, new

—*Maria Mankin*

• •• •

FOR A WOMAN STRUGGLING WITH INFERTILITY

I pray with you the prayers of Hannah, the prayers for a child, prayers for
that re-creation of the world in another's tender eyes, for the heart of love
to beat in your home.

And in the meantime, I pray for you:
    Patience times a million
    Sleep that rests you
    Friends who listen
    Kind doctors
    Laughter with your beloved
    And trust
    That the heart of love will find you
    By God's grace.

—*Amy Sens*

• •• •

God of the Newborn,
It's midnight, 1:42 AM, 2:56 AM, 4:17 AM and it's getting light.
    I've been up all night, walking the floorboards, humming that same song,
rocking like a crazy aunt, crick in my neck from holding that one position

lest the baby start crying again. Remind me that sleep makes everything possible, and send more of it into our house. Remind me that these days are precious, yes, but I don't have to love every minute of them. Remind me that someday, someday, this baby will sleep through the night, and help me to hold on until that day.

—*Molly Phinney Baskette*

•◦◦•

PRAYER FOR A MOTHER ANTICIPATING GIVING UP HER BIRTH CHILD

Let us hold in our hearts _____ , who is preparing to give up her
    soon-to-be-born child.
In her courage and her sorrow, her despair and her hope,
May the gift of her child become a blessing of love for her, the child,
    the new parents.
May she be surrounded by love and peace.
    This is our prayer.

—*Lynne Frith*

•◦◦•

Amy shares her moment before writing prayer: "I prepared by meditating on John 1:1. In the beginning was the Word, and the Word was with God, and the Word was God":

FOR A WOMAN WHO HAS MISCARRIED

God, what is your word?
The beginning has come to the end
joy and hope are now
    lost and forgotten
God, speak a word of peace now.

—*Amy Sens*

•⬚•

Devoree says, of her preparation, "It is most important to trust that God will be part of the process. I also am mindful that there may disappointment. The prayer is for God to strengthen the parents to be":

Loving God, please continue to bless these dear persons who wish to share their love and by extension your love with a child who needs parents. We trust that your hand will guide. Bless the child who will come into this new family. As they move through the adoption/fostering process, help them to be ready and also prepared to face whatever may come. If they are not to have children at this time, let them find comfort in their disappointment. If their family is increased, give them the tools, skills, patience, and wisdom to be the best parents they can be.

—*Devoree Clifton Crist*

•⬚•

FOR A PERSON/COUPLE WHO DOES NOT WISH TO RAISE CHILDREN

Am I defective, my Mother-Father God? I love kids—their cries,
their curious eyes—but my generativity is elsewhere.
Am I broken? All around me rejoice in new life (at least this form with its
    tiny toes). And
then they turn to me . . . and all I can say to their raised eyebrows is: No.
Seed in me new life, Creating God. But not that way.

—*Sharon Benton*

•⬚•

FOR A BIRTH PARENT

Do you know what it's like
to put your child,
your baby,

your love into someone else's hands, God?
Do you know what it's like
to see their face in every child,
in every teen,
in every young adult,
as years go by?
Do you know what it's like
to wonder "what if,"
or "will I,"
or "do they"?
I hope so, God.
Oh, God . . . I hope so.

—*Richard Bott*

Praying for a distant friend, e-mailing an in-law of a relative, remembering that request mentioned on Sunday morning—this reaching, this extension of the self into the lives of others, opens up a new conduit in conversation with God. Praying into an unfamiliar situation, or with a person who may be practically a stranger, prepares us for the challenges that may still lie ahead on our own paths.

Praying, praying, praying hard that your body is feeling better.
That the body aches are leaving, the cough settling, the yucky nose drying.
The small and expert team of neutrophils swimming and fighting off all
    those virus germs.
Praying, praying, praying your spirit hit bottom yesterday and now you've
    pushed off with both strong spirit feet.
Kicking and swimming to the top of this Christmas Eve Day.
Just in time to see the Star, hear the Angels, make eye contact with a Baby
    and acknowledge the Summons.
No matter where you are.

And praying, praying, demanding, praying that you get to experience all of
that in the comfort of your home surrounded by your children and family.

—*Sue B. Donnelly*

• ⚅ •

"I start 'O God . . .' and proceed to describe what I see." Alan Parker continues,
"Prayers spring forth: for a young girl looking out the back window of the school
bus and making faces at me; for the man in the pickup ahead of me, its muffler
dragging on the pavement; or a prayer about the beauty (or ugliness) I see as I
look at a house or the glorious hills in the distance. There is no end to the prayers
that arise—prayers of gratitude, tears, hope, plea, and delight. They're short
prayers, with time for wordless prayer within and after the words. Most of these
prayers are never written down":

God, thank you for the bus ahead of me, and the goofy face pressed to the
back window, waving and grinning. May she always be well. Thank you for
reminding me to wave back at her.

—*Alan F. Parker*

• ⚅ •

God, I'm nervous for what's next—work, volunteering, grad school, paying
off loans, becoming an adult, making new friends. Give me peace.

—*Cody E. Maynus*

• ⚅ •

A PRAYER FROM SOUTH AFRICA

Dear Lord,
You know Lolo and how he is filled with anger,
You know his story:
No father;
mother died of AIDS;
brought up in the sheltered home of his grandmother's employer;
then suddenly thrust into life in the townships;
no friends;
but being bullied and harassed by other children:
Lord, he is so angry,
he feels so alone,
he feels so helpless.
Open his eyes so that he can see
that you are there for him,
his father, his mother,
his friend, his career,
his protector.
Take the anger from him;
give him an alternative way for being,
so that he can grow and flourish. Amen.

—*Isobel de Gruchy*

God, that child who just got off the bus; you know him, right? His backpack looks heavy. Is he walking into a safe and loving home? If so, thank you. If not, how can I help?

—*Alan F. Parker*

"I carry a pad of 'little yellow stickies' with me everywhere," LL Kroouze DuBreuil reports. What I find myself doing is pulling them out when I see a prayer concern. I feel empathy for people in unexpected situations because I find myself in such situations. And the stickies are the right size and feel for these impromptu prayers":

I see her walking along the side of the road with her Walgreens bag.
God, walk with her and all other tired travelers.

—*LL Kroouze DuBreuil*

•🎞•

RIDING ON THE BUS IN THE CBD (Central Business District, Auckland)

I give thanks for the man singing on the bus.
May he find companions to share his happiness,
and to be beside him when he is down.
May he be touched with love.
Let the richness of his voice and his friendly nature
lift the spirits of other passengers.

—*Lynne Frith*

•🎞•

COFFEEHOUSE PRAYER

Holy Poet, whose stanzas are the lights of heaven
and who is on the slam circuit with Jeremiah and Amos,
stand with that vulnerable young woman
at the open mic—her first time
and a sonnet in her hand.
In the beginning
we are all reading the Word. Amen.

—*Maren Tirabassi*

•🎞•

God be with us in this in-between time. In between school and summer, in between current homes and new homes, in between current job and new jobs, in between current community and new community, in between old life and new life. Jesus walked the walk of an in-between-er. The ultimate in-between-er. And he did it with grace and poise and love. Help us figure out who he is and how he did it and let us do it with grace and love as we pray like he did for our own community. God, hear these prayers.

—*Christy Ackley Zuzelo*

• •• •

Diane Lamoureux Ciba wrote this as a Facebook post before it became a reflection for this book, before it emerged in prayer for all those who receive care and give it:

"Although I have journeyed with those nearing the end of their days several times in the past, it is a much different struggle to be the primary caregiver and 'decider' for a sibling. When my brother struggled with the after-effects of a stroke, he turned to me for help and I took on a role that I could not have imagined. I cared for him for 16 months, traveling 200 miles at least once a week. His gratitude and good humor made it possible, but there were days when I did not think I could take another negative comment. So this is my prayer for all caregivers, spoken from my place of need":

Striving for balance and living the challenge, bring peace to my brother as I
    care for him each day. Amen.
Difficult choices, clamoring needs, conflicting voices, Caregiving God,
    help me sift and decide based on what's best for him, not me. Amen.
Opinions of others shadow my thoughts. Release me from those voices;
    free me from "woulda, coulda, shoulda." Amen.
Thanks be to God for strength for the journey, patience in its unfolding,
    wisdom and compassion. Let me be filled with your Spirit. Amen.

—*Diane Lamoureux Ciba*

• •• •

Addictions take a terrible toll, whether they are addictions of substance or of process. Alcohol, drugs, and gambling used to be the addictions most often named, but there are many more. In a digital age, addictions based in Internet use include pornography, spending/shopping, and the inability to leave the online world.

PRAYER OF ONE SUFFERING IN ADDICTION

Addiction's grip is strong, O God.
I cry to You for freedom.
Strengthen me to break my chains.
Lead me to wholeness and peace.

—*Jerry Hebenstreit*

MARY'S LAMENT

In the night I cry for him
O my son, O my son
as one in a darkened afternoon
for her son cried

This place of addiction
transfixed to screen and keys
Why do you look on these who can never love you
in your search for peace

In the sun and under bluest sky
I cry O my son with a bottle
for comfort, a bench for a bed as the wait continues
for night to return

O my son where will you go
So far from me, and

when did you leave, for you slipped away
my son, like a prayer lost in my heart

—*Erice C. Fairbrother*

•👓•

I know he is trying, God,
oh, do I know . . .
but on the days when the alcohol
reeks in his pores, when he won't meet my eyes
because he knows that I know that he has slipped again,
when I am shaken and sick and furious
at this burden he has to bear,
I ask myself why you don't do more.
I am hoarse from asking you to do more
or to show me what I might do.
I am tired, God, of being so afraid for him.
I am tired of waiting for your grace to appear.

—*Maria Mankin*

•👓•

PRAYER FROM AA

In the solitude of this empty day,
without apparent company and surrounded by ghosts,
embraced by fears and surrounded by oblivion,
I want to put my injured life in your hands, good God.
With unsteady step and trembling voice,
overcast eyes and moist hands,
I seek to offer my fragility, anchor my broken spirit,
settle my restless mind and body, tired of blows.
In the depths of the glass,
I dreamed to find calm,

sip by sip I drank away the time
and between my fingers my life slipped away.
In my omnipotent vanity
I built myself a world of illusions;
I believed, surely I believed, that this was the way
toward some sort of happiness.
Today, deep in my soul, nothing remains;
no friends to greet, family to share with, tears to weep ...
Only this hollow feeling that shakes me,
that awakens me, that sparks me
and that pushes me to seek you,
to believe in you, to love you, to dream of you
and to drink you
not at the bottom of the glass
but here
in the depths of myself.

ORACIÓN DE UN AA

En la soledad de este día vacío,
sin compañía aparente y rodeado de fantasmas,
abrazado de miedos
y circundado de olvidos,
quiero poner mi vida lastimada
en tus manos de Dios bueno.
Con paso inseguro y con voz temblorosa,
los ojos nublados y las manos húmedas,
busco sostener mi fragilidad,
dónde anclar mi espíritu quebrado,
dónde reposar mi mente inquieta
y mi cuerpo cansado de golpes.
En el fondo del cristal
soñé encontrar la calma,

sorbo a sorbo me fui bebiendo el tiempo
y entre los dedos se me escurrió la vida.
En mi vanidad omnipotente
me construí un mundo de ilusiones;
creí, ciertamente creí, que éste era el camino
hacia alguna suerte de felicidad.
Hoy, en la profundidad del alma,
no me queda nada;
tampoco quedan amigos para saludar
ni familia con la que compartir
ni lágrimas que llorar ...
Sólo esta sensación hueca que me sacude,
que me despierta,
que me provoca
y que me empuja
a buscarte,
a creerte,
a amarte,
a soñarte
y a beberte
no en el fondo del cristal
sino aquí,
en el fondo de mi mismo.

—*Gerardo C. C. Oberman*

PETERUS

Lord,
He carries and will always carry the sin of his mother.
He lives with foetal alcohol syndrome.
He tries so hard to learn:
Give him perseverance.

He tries so hard to please:
Give him dignity.
He bears his family's mockery:
Give him endurance.
He knows his limitations:
Give him new abilities.
He wants to do more:
Be with him, within him, and help him to grow.

—*Isobel de Gruchy*

• •• •

We who are the psalmists of our day have not inhabited all the experiences about which we speak. We have two gifts—memory and empathy—and with these, we write prayers. Matthew Braddock describes how he came to write the following prayer:

"'I Hate My Job' had its genesis in my own experiences of heartache and soul decay heading to work as if I were walking to a guillotine. I first had this experience years ago, fixing boat propellers in South Boston. Abused, bullied, ignored, or dehumanized, it is hard to imagine healing. All I wanted was to stay true to my core values and find a new job. As I listen to others, sit in a coffee shop, or watch commuters on the DC Metro, I think many feel the same way."

These next prayers are loosely connected with issues of employment, the lack of employment and human hopes around employment.

I HATE MY JOB

My trip to work feels like a journey to my death.
    Or, at least to a daily dose of torment.
I die five days a week,
    suffering the bites from the swarm of workers around me.
I hate my job. I really do.
My fantasy? A job where my soul doesn't ache and decay;
    a workplace where I'm treated like a human being.

I hate that my job makes me an angry person.
I fly home and take the stings of my day out on family and friends.
They hate my job, too.

I hate feeling trapped. There's nothing else out there.
I can't quit without having something else in place.

God, help me breathe deeply and find hope,
    sustenance in the wilderness,
    renewal of some joy.
Give me strength.
And help me not to act like those whom I dread every day at work.

—*Matthew Braddock*

• •• •

First day, first hour, sitting in front of a strange keyboard, in a strange place,
surrounded by strange people . . .
In this time and place, God be with me—root for me—please!

—*LL Kroouze DuBreuil*

• •• •

This is a test. Only a test.
It measures where I am and how far I have to go.
It cannot measure who I am. I am your beloved.
Thank you for the reminder, God-of-trial-and-error.
This is only a test.

—*Sharon Benton*

• •• •

SHADES OF EMPLOYMENT GRAY

We pray for all whose employment situation
puts words to their lives and erodes their self-respect.

for "laid-off" who feel like the dirty laundry of employees,
for "furloughed" who can't remember requesting
to feed their families only three days a week,
for the "underemployed,"
defined by themselves or others,
some dollar amount on their check
or the head-to-hand ratio,

and for the "job market,"
as if everyone who really wanted
could pick up the biggest brightest pumpkin of a job
their kids could help carry home.

"Fired" has some heat in it!
God, fire the way our culture equates
human value with money and work,
fire those who profit
from the suffering of their neighbors,
fire those who enjoy many benefits
while undermining collective bargaining,
and remind us all of some old good language,
like "making a living." Amen.

—*Maren Tirabassi*

• ◼◼ •

PRAYER FOR THE SERVICE WORKERS IN A FOOD COURT

Let us give thanks for those who clean up after our meals—
Who remove trays of dirty dishes,
Who wipe tables,
Who mop floors.

May tired shoulders and aching feet be rested and soothed.
May rosters be fair and just wages be paid.
May those who serve also know the blessing of being served.

—*Lynne Frith*

•••

Faithful God, the cycle of poverty is difficult to break. If the uncertainty of navigating a job search isn't enough, the shame of so frequently being at the mercy of others is an equally incredible wound to overcome. Soothe famished spirits and shrinking stomachs with the daily bread that each needs for a new, life-giving cycle to emerge. Amen.

—*Jeff Nelson*

•••

In the office, she is completely composed,
frustration tucked away beneath her own expectations.
She keeps her chin up and resumé ready,

ready for the next step, the opportunity to take
that massive leap of faith. She is anxious
to move past these 9-to-5 paychecks into work
that asks more, gives more, means more.

She is poised on the brink now, God,
only seeking the courage promised
to live into your word.

—*Maria Mankin*

•••

THE FALLEN LEADER

God,
He was bright and ambitious;
He wielded power;
He called the shots,
And his underlings did his bidding.
He was a demi-god, an orator
Who roused the base emotions of the
Disgruntled have-nots
Against the Enemy—those who have.
(and he was one who had—and had plenty).
He grabbed at power—more and more,
He was ruthless in its pursuit,
Till he was brought crashing down,
Calling "foul" and "I'm innocent."

Lord, help him to see himself,
Help him to rise up again,
But a changed person.

—*Isobel de Gruchy*

PRAYER FOR A PERSON WHO IS QUITTING

Giver of Gifts, you have granted each of us gifts, skills, and talents that we are to share with others through our work. At this time, (person's name) is moving from one setting into a new and different setting. Give guidance and wisdom. Offer hope and promise. Allow peace and stillness. Let this new opportunity be a place where (person's name) can be a part of a team that shares respect and encouragement. Allow this change of places of employment, provide empowerment and enlivenment so that (person's name) can be a productive member of a new team, where his/her gifts will be recognized, honored, and appreciated. Amen.

—*Mary Beth Hartenstein*

• 🎲 •

Lynne Frith writes, "I have a practice related to living under the flight path for helicopters to the hospital near by. Whenever I hear a helicopter approaching the hospital I silently offer a brief prayer for the person being transported, his/her relatives, the paramedics, and helicopter pilot and crew":

May the skill of flight crew and paramedics keep the patient safe.
May the skill of medical staff and health workers restore the patient to health.
Where the injury or illness is fatal, may death be peaceful.
May family and friends be surrounded with love, and filled with courage and hope. Amen.

—*Lynne Frith*

• 🎲 •

What other prayers do we have because of where we live, the corner we pass by walking the dog, the building beside our workplace, the modes of transportation we take? With how many such silent and brief prayers could we surround people?

I can't help but notice this father kneeling
to cling to his son for another moment before
the plane boards. His camo does anything
but make him invisible in this crowded terminal,
and his posture begs forgiveness from the child
he leaves behind. The stiff nonchalance
set in his son's narrow shoulders—this is not the first time
he has said goodbye here, or watched his father leave
to protect the lives of boys halfway around the world
rather than stay home where he might save his own
from the constant aching fear of not knowing
if this is the day his father will die.

God, be with them both. Be with this worn down
soldier and this brittle son. Carve this, the moment

of hesitant love, into each of their hearts to carry
with them on the uncertain road ahead. Amen.

—*Maria Mankin*

● ●● ●

AT AN AIRPORT TERMINAL—Prayer for a soldier with a folded flag in hand

God, be with the soldier who waits alone by an unmarked door near Arrivals.
He stands tall, with a folded flag cradled in his arms. Is he waiting for a fallen
friend? Is he waiting for a grieving family? Be with him as his lips quiver beneath the visor of a sturdy cap. Be with him as he musters courage to form
the words "on behalf of a grateful nation" with steadiness, and as he reaches
out his arms in offering.

—*Elizabeth D. Barnum*

● ●● ●

The Bible is filled with immigrants and refugees, people who are crossing borders
in hope or with fear, who may meet welcome or intolerance. These are prayers for
travelers and contemporary crossers of borders.

Matthew Braddock reflects on the personal experience that shapes his prayer.
"I have worked in Washington, D.C., as a faith advocate for the Uniting American
Families Act. This legislation would allow gay and lesbian citizens to sponsor their
spouses' citizenship. Right now, many partners are deported, or their visas are not
renewed. They are forced to choose between the risk of staying here illegally, moving abroad, or splitting their families. I listened to stories of immigrants who pay
taxes, donate money, do essential jobs, and seek happiness—just like native-born
people. I reflected on scripture about 'resident aliens,' 'strangers and sojourners,'
and 'the foreigners among you.' God calls the nations to generous hospitality,
equality, compassion, and fair treatment for all":

STRUGGLING WITH IMMIGRATION

I'm trying to live my life, do the right thing,
  support my family and be a good citizen.

But what about the "sojourners and strangers" I see in my community?
We live together, yet inhabit different worlds:
 field workers and parking lot attendants,
 day laborers lined up for work at the home improvement store,
 men nailing shingles on roofs and running lawn mowers,
 women selling roses at the street corner,
 the nurse at the retirement home who cares for elders,
 those who follow their hearts to America to be with their true loves.
Are all these immigrants really taking jobs from Americans? Avoiding taxes?
Living in luxury?
Are they trying to live their lives, do right, support families,
 and be good citizens?

Most of us have an immigrant story:
 some "sojourners and strangers" in our layered past.
That's why you, God, invite us to remember . . .
 where we came from,
 how we got here,
 and how to show hospitality, fairness, and love.
God of Boundless Compassion,
 what's one thing I can do today to expand the borders of my love
 for all people?

—*Matthew Braddock*

• ■ •

BEDTIME PRAYER

Holy Wanderer, who had no place to lay your head, tuck in tonight your
motel children, the welfare ones and all the others, your shelter-children,
your sleeping-in-the-airport because-the-flight-is-delayed children, your liv-
ing-rough children, even your cell, dormitory, hospital room children, too,
that all may find within that you are home. Amen.

—*Maren Tirabassi*

• •• •

PRAYER OF AN IMMIGRANT

In this land I am a stranger.
In Your love I am at home.
O God, help me find peace and welcome here.

—*Jerry Hebenstreit*

• •• •

God without walls, who says . . .
"come unto me all who are weary
and have no documents
for my asylum is easy
and my green is valley . . . and card,"
shelter all your children
from ICE-broken doors, predators-at-law,
and the day of deportation,
so that sanctuaries can return to being
dusty old places with pews. Amen.

—*Maren Tirabassi*

• •• •

PRAYER FOR A PERSON WHO IS HOMESICK FOR ANOTHER COUNTRY

God, be with the woman who leans against the airport terminal windowpane
with boarding pass in left hand, carry-on bag perched on her right forearm. As
she waits to depart on the red-eye flight, catch the tears that fall behind the
sunglasses she still wears at this late hour. The screen at the gate reads north-
east, the ankle-length black wool coat reads winter . . . and grief. Be the ground
beneath her feet as she steps off the plane tomorrow morning just after sunrise.
No matter how far away from home she may feel, accompany her home.

—*Elizabeth D. Barnum*

Jeff Nelson says, "When I write prayers, I try to think of a few situations that I've been familiar with in ministry—what is described in words and in body language. I try to be specific and brief, and to be realistic and hopeful."

Although we challenge ourselves by imagining the pain, suffering, or celebration of others, we also all need to come back, at times, to the experience of praying what we know. There will always be a place for this in our practice, and these prayers will always come out of a strength we might not even realize we possess. We have all survived some experiences, and we are all in the midst of surviving others; in those dark times, prayer—for ourselves or for others facing the same struggles—is what we can cling to and rejoice in. It is always, always available, no matter the hour or circumstances.

PRAYER IN DANGER

God met in the two AM white-out
who does not fling the snow under our tires
blind the windshield,
vanish highway lines, road signs,
and the ominous shape of toll booths,
please cover these hands
gripping the steering wheel,

and, in all our sudden times of fear,
give us truck taillights to follow
or a shoulder where we can pull off to wait.
Fire and hail, snow and frost,
stormy wind . . . you are there, too. Amen.

—*Maren Tirabassi*

Among our prayers are those for dysfunctions in the church. The first one that follows is a prayer for someone who has been damaged emotionally, physically, or spiritually in a setting of faith. The second responds to deep problems in the community of faith itself. The last reminds us of the hope that awaits us when we feel safe walking into any of God's homes.

Greater than we can ask or imagine?
Greater than we can ask or imagine.
Greater than we can ask or imagine!
Christ's love for us—
broken and whole.
In the church . . . and . . .
in spite of the church.
Christ's love—
broken and whole.

—Richard Bott

Erice's words introduce us to this prayer. "This describes how parish ministry can feel when there is refusal to change. 'Like a stone rolling away' is perhaps a rather faith-empty allusion to the empty tomb—which I am beginning to think represents more and more true emptiness. Maybe resurrection in some way talks more about emptiness than fulfillment. Ezekiel, after all, was having a vision—in parish ministry I am looking at real bones":

IN THE VALLEY OF BONES

I looked on the face of the dead
And they said
We are dead
We are dead

I looked on the face of the dead
And I said

You will live
You will live

I heard my voice echo
like a stone
rolling away
into silence

—*Erice C. Fairbrother*

• •• •

PRAYER FOR MANY MANSIONS

God, sweet as charoset,
complex as the nine-pointed star of Baha'i,
deep as salah,
cut your cross in our hearts
so that our intolerance pours away
and we are open to
the beautiful and many
ways your children worship. Amen.

—*Maren Tirabassi*

• •• •

There comes a time for each of us when we desperately need to pray about and for love. Romantic love, familial love, the love of a dear friend, or the struggle to let go of love that is damaging us—so many relationships take up room in our hearts, it's natural that we offer up our blessings, fears, and struggles to God. Love can be sweet and funny and terrifying and exhausting. It can whittle us down to our essence, and it can build us back up.

A Cherokee legend retold on Tumblr speaks well to this great dichotomy. In the story, a grandmother tells her grandson, "Two wolves live inside me, as they do in each of us. One is anger, sorrow, regret, inferiority—the other, love, joy, peace, and hope.

These two are in constant struggle with each other." The child considers this, and then asks her, "But which of these wolves will win the fight?" She answers, "The one I feed."

The prayers we share, and the ones we hold silently, deep within our hearts, are the soul food we offer God in our own struggle to let the respectful, forgiving, self-loving wolf win.

God, love is messy. We have had our hearts broken. We have stayed up late imagining futures with someone and wakened to realize that life doesn't pattern itself after our dreams. We have let our lusting and our latching-on turn people into prizes to be won or bounty to be protected. Go with us as we learn to see people the way you see them: not as sex symbols, not as tools, not as stepping stools or tokens, but as dearly loved children. Forgive us for the ways we have hurt others, heal the broken places inside us, and let our fractured, faltering love come, bit by bit, to mirror your perfect love.

—*Lindsay Ruth Popper*

My grandmother and I curve together,
alone in the midst of this hospital's hustle. She leans in
to hear the words we wrote for the wedding she won't see.

She has already given me the gifts I need though, in the witness of
    her own marriage,
with its endurance of struggle and rebirth. She has clothed me with
    her gentleness,
her iron will, her sense of justice. She has wreathed my head with
    her lessons of forgiveness
and unflappable love. She has wrapped me, finally, in her spirit,
    fierce and beautiful and bright.

This woman, tiny and bent now in her chair,
she has dressed my soul for a strong marriage.
Patiently, and for many years, she has written

and rewritten these words we will speak
on my wild and trusting heart.

—*Maria Mankin*

•••

FOR A PERSON ENTERING AN ARRANGED MARRIAGE

Let us hold _____ in our hearts, whose marriage has been arranged by
    her/his parents.
May she/he and her/his fiancé(e), _____ , grow in knowledge, respect, and
    love for each other,
That their lives together may be marked by harmony, trust, generosity, and
    love.
This is our prayer.

—*Lynne Frith*

•••

A PRAYER FOR A PERSON WHO HAS EXPERIENCED THE DISINTEGRATION OF A RELATIONSHIP

Oh God of Love,
How difficult it can be to absorb rejection.
How difficult it can be to accept failure.
How difficult it can be to acknowledge anger.
Envelop _____ in your love,
For in your love, bitterness and despair melt away,
And even broken webs are held before the hope of your future.

—*Lina Andronoviene*

•••

O God of Compassion and Mercy,
Carla stands on the corner of hopelessness and despair
The pain that comes from betrayal
The hands designed for love
became the hands that bruised
and broke bones
Trapped . . .
The pills in the medicine cabinet beckon
Offering sweet relief from fear and pain
Help her to know she is your beloved . . . she's not alone
There are those waiting to help . . . wanting
To listen and hear
That while ending her life may seem the easiest answer
In the end it is not the only answer
Your love can give her the strength
To stand up to him . . . see her belovedness
Your love can give her confidence
To be free and have new life

—*Carol Hallman*

God of Love,
It's time to leave. Give me the courage to leave, and the tools I need.
A friend, a safe house, some money, the fortitude to stay away,
    when I miss my lover so much, or fear the future alone even more
    than the fear of staying.
Help me to love myself even a little bit more than I love my lover,
    so I can have myself for a lifetime.

—*Molly Phinney Baskette*

Devoree Crist talks about "the grief associated with loss of a home. Not only is it connected with so many memories, but if the change is unexpected or unwanted, it only compounds the sense of loss. I want this prayer to be one of reassurance. It is God who holds these people and cares for them through a tough time":

Dear God of All,
Please be with _____ as he/she/they face the loss of their home. There is so much tied to a home that it is not a simple of matter of giving up a geographical location. Please, Holy One, hold them in your embrace as they experience the grief and guide them through it to a new place where they can once again make a home and feel safe and move forward with their lives.

—*Devoree Clifton Crist*

FOR A PERSON WHO HAS SURVIVED A STORM

Gone. Home, possessions, memories,
lost in a sudden bitter wind.
But we survive.
By Your grace, that will be enough to carry on.

—*Jerry Hebenstreit*

PRAYER FOR A ROUGH SLEEPER ON A RAINY DAY

May this man find shelter from the stormy weather;
may his cardboard and sleeping bag remain dry through the night.
May he receive gifts of hospitality and loving, compassionate care,
so that his stormy life may also be calmed.
    This my prayer.

—*Lynne Frith*

"So I start a sentence at that moment, 'O God . . .' and proceed to describe what I see. Prayers spring forth . . ."

God, if my daughter were murdered as Melissa was, I'd lose my mind. I knew her a little; even so, I'm losing it. Help me cry and remember—even the broken souls who killed her.

—*Alan F. Parker*

• ◦◦ •

FOR A PERSON WHO IS COMING TO TERMS WITH SEXUAL VIOLATION

She has kept her secret for ten years, Hidden God,
you the only one who's had her back. Fearfully,
now she names his terrorizing; discloses her history
to parents and friends. Help them have her back, too,
as you have—in secret—so long.

—*Sharon Benton*

• ◦◦ •

We could say that prisons are full of murderers, rapists, liars, and thieves. We could say that they are full of guards and wardens and officers. Really though, prisons are full of human beings. God, help us to look in prisons and see Jesus, who became fully human to show us how to be fully human. Help those on both sides of the cell doors remember their humanity and the humanity of those around them. Soften hearts, Lord. Bring healing. Compel those of us on the outside to extend your love to our incarcerated brothers and sisters; shield prison workers from becoming calloused; enable offenders to grow and change; and help everyone to see all people as people, dearly loved by you, the God who made every one of us in your image.

—*Lindsay Ruth Popper*

• ◦◦ •

God, my brother is about to go to jail. He did something really bad. Can I forgive him? I know you will, but you're different from me. Or are you? Help me out here, God . . .

—*Alan F. Parker*

• •• •

God, my mind is racing and my heart is pounding. Calm the turbulent sea of my life. Move earlier maybe. Help me be still and know you.

—*Cody E. Maynus*

• •• •

At times, we have to face dangers that have no possibility of conviction or redemption. We may have to stare in the darkness on our own, or beside a friend, and strain to imagine a glimmer of light.

FOR A PERSON SUFFERING WITH DEPRESSION

Submerged in waves of depression,
the surface a dim shadow, arms too tired, soul too weary to try.
Rescue me, God. Lead me to the light.

This loneliness is a wall, O God.
No way over, now way out, no way through on my own.
I need Your strength and help.

—*Jerry Hebenstreit*

• •• •

FOR A PERSON WHO LOVES SOMEONE THINKING ABOUT SUICIDE

"Out of the deep
I cry to you"—yes! The deep,
God. He drags me under

in his depression. So be—(I AM)—
his lifeline. All I know to do
is throw you
toward him
and hold on.

—*Sharon Benton*

Dead God, paused as the Passover moon
in the western morning sky,
visit now those who live with depression,
remind them you
know
this
emptiness
and raise them with you—
up, up. Amen.

—*Maren Tirabassi*

FOR A PERSON WHOSE FRIEND HAS COMMITTED SUICIDE

She left a bitter hole when she took her life.
Help me, God, to fill the hole with love, not anger,
with fond remembrance, not rejection.

There's a hole in my heart.
I wasn't able to help him or stop him.
All I can do is grieve.
Lead me to hope, O God. Turn mourning to joy.

—*Jerry Hebenstreit*

• ▣ •

IN SICKNESS

All night, God, I pray for you to take away this pain.
I make elaborate bargains, all the things I'll do
better, and for others,

if you just let me rest. When finally I sleep, dreams push
from my mind all the things I have promised. I am no better.
I have practiced no greater compassion. I deserved that pain

because I am still me—a frail human spirit inside this vulnerable
compromised body. *No, you whisper, no. I am not the God of pain,*
or retribution for broken promises. I am the God of finally resting.
Of starting over. Of making promises. Of trying to keep them.

I am the God who loves you, frail, vulnerable, compromised.

—*Maria Mankin*

• ▣ •

The following is an e-mail blessing sent from one of the contributors in this book
to another, and yes, an e-mail most certainly can be prayer-full.

Thinking about how birds and creatures make it through this long, cold winter. How some little creature is snuggled in your discarded hair. How our
losses, when shared, strengthen each other's resistance to our own challenges
seen and unseen. Thinking about how I'm soooo happy that you are almost
done with infusion and how we'll never be the same after this year.

Your DNA may be objectively and forever changed from chemo and your
hair may grow back shockingly white or blond or curly. And something in
all of us who love you is forever changed too. Is it our DNA? Maybe. Your
silky threads of wisdom, honesty, hope, pain, joy, and love are woven forever

into our hearts and minds. Can't wait to say farewell to chemo and hello to spring and recovery.

—*Sue B. Donnelly*

• •• •

PRAYER FOR A WOMAN WITHOUT MEDICAL COVERAGE

God, you designed the awesome anus, and the bright elastic rectum of the baby in diapers and the prune-and-flax-packing traveler. We praise you for sphincters like flute stops and the labyrinth of intestines more prayerful than any replica of Chartres.

Hold in your love this woman without health benefits who decided the price of a colonoscopy weighed against rent and food, her son's toothache, daughter's wrist broken on the ice, the glasses needed for driving, was too high (besides, she heard all the joke-whining of people with insurance about the inconvenient prep).

Nobody but you, God, loved her colon, and now this silent, undetected cancer is shortening her life, and costing everyone so much, especially those kids with mouths to kiss and hands to hold.
Her bag is sweet to you and her life is precious.

Shit?
Jesus defined it as the laws of the tight-hearted, not what goes down the drain. Wipe it away. Amen.

—*Maren Tirabassi*

• •• •

Devoree Crist spent time meditating on prayers for those who are facing illness: "I consider a person facing an illness that may have no cure. In asking for healing I focus on strength to handle the diagnosis, hope that it is a manageable illness and that centering on God will provide comfort, and improvement or the courage to live with a situation. In all prayer I recognize that God is always present and that it is our turning to God that opens our minds, hearts, spirits."

A PRAYER FOR A PERSON DEALING WITH CHRONIC DISEASE SUCH AS FIBROMYALGIA

Having a "non-disease"
Yet not being able to do what you should be able to do—
others do it without problems, after all
But at least now some recognition
That what this is not just imagination
Or laziness
Or craziness . . .
Lord, help us to learn
To rest in you,
Content to move
Just step by step
Knowing
That our worth does not depend
On what we do.
We simply are,
And we are
Because of your grace.

—*Lina Andronoviene*

This is a prayer about names, but also about far more than that . . .

Dear God, Creator, Son and Spirit,
When I was a child I was taught a rhyme—"Sticks and stones may break my bones but names, they will never hurt me." As a child, I told myself it was true. As an adult I know it is not true. Name-calling is one of the cruelest forms of torture. As an adult who knows only too well the pain of the depths of a clinical depression, the despair and physical panic of anxiety, who knows

the feeling of having been on the wrong side of a locked door and as an adult who willingly takes medication that addles the brain, I know the agony of being called names only too well.

Holy God, I try every day to thank you for the advancement of medical science that gives me the quality of life that I have. I thank you with all my heart. I pray for mercy, mercy please, for those who call me "looney," "a sicko," "a druggie," "mad." It is hard to ignore these words, hard to hear the insults.

Help me. Please help me to love the people who, because of their lack of understanding or their fear of mental illness, use these cruel words. Help me to love, not to hate.

God have mercy, Christ have mercy, God have mercy.
Amen.

—A. Heather Kelly

PRAYER FOR A PERSON WHO IS TRYING TO MAKE A NEW IDENTITY, POSTSTROKE

God, whose incarnation divided time in two, BC Before Christ and AD Anno Domini, be present and known to the man who sits in the rehabilitation wing waiting for the physical therapist. His life, too, is two parts—two halves—two movements—two acts. Prestroke and poststroke. That there is even a "post-" he declares as a stroke of luck. There is nothing about this that feels like AD the year of the Lord, other than being slave to the appointments of relearning walking and talking, of relearning vision and voice. BCE Before the Common Era and CE the Common Era. There is nothing that feels common about this "post-" era in which he lives. He wonders, "How can I be set apart as a poster-child for miracles when I feel so much pain?" Rather, he yearns to be a child of your mystery, of your healing, of your love, of the prayer you utter again and again to begin again, begin again, begin again.

—Elizabeth D. Barnum

• ◳ •

PRAYER OF ONE WHO HAS LEARNED THAT A DIAGNOSIS IS A TERMINAL ONE

Life. Death. I did not think those two words would come so close together. I had such hope that the words spoken by the doctor would be different. I feel lost. How do I move from living with my illness to dying from my disease? I will need all of your help, all of your strength, all of your courage to do this. Companion me, Holy One, into this time when I will struggle to hold on to the life that I have and yet deal with the death that awaits me. Let me know that you are near.

—*Mary Beth Hartenstein*

• ◳ •

God, she has spent nights pacing, panicking, sweating in pain
for hours on her own. She has told no one, until tonight,
of the unsuccessful tests, the days of work missed,
the hollow fear eating away at the edge of everything she does.

She has stayed silent, God, because she wasn't sure any of us would care
enough to listen to her long story with its inconclusive ending.
She has been alone through months of doctors' appointments
and failed treatments because of us, because we have not shown
enough patience or compassion to earn her trust.

Please, God, please forgive us this hurrying, shallow love—our constant
    faith failing—
that keeps us from treating strangers, and friends, and even family
as the precious and worthwhile children of God we know them to be.

—*Maria Mankin*

• ◳ •

Hope you are feeling the power today—
your own remarkable, awe-inspiring power and
the power of all those concentric circles of individuals praying, praying, praying
the power of years of dedicated research scientists bent over microscopes
the power of all the Ewings survivors who have paved the way before you
the power of those who will walk later in your beautiful footprints
the power of your family and your friends
the power of the holy name of Jesus who will sit with you today
the power of time that heals all wounds.

Praying you into and through this cycle with no surprises, just tried and true transcendentalist skills. You are totally doing this.

May the infusion room be filled with real Light and real people.
Beautiful humans, battered and bruised and hopeful and loved.
May you receive the healing Light today at least half as much as you put out.

—*Sue B. Donnelly*

• ◑◑ •

At one time or another, each of us must taste the bitterness of grief. This great loss is a terrible thing, but it is also what binds us together. It is the universal experience, reflected differently in each of us, but nonetheless, shared. We must reflect on all of grief's stages, if only because we have no choice. We are not eternal; we are fragile, vulnerable, deeply loved.

THE WIDOW'S PSALM

O God of love, why is this world so empty?
So empty of Your Spirit?
The ring of a cell phone rips my life apart.
"He was found on the ground," it said.
Dead air behind, then nothing . . . nothing.
A box devoid of life, devoid of connection.
Emptiness where I once could always hear his voice.

I reach out and nothing is there;
No voice, no form, no love—all gone.
A technology of convenience turns hard to stark plastic.
No presence with which to share humanness,
No flesh to cry on, no eyes to find You behind.

O God of love, I praise You with all that You made me.
I call and You answer me. Me?
As startled by Your presence as that death-filled ring;
I answer, without real comprehension.
You speak to me words I understand but cannot translate.
There is no dead air—but life, blessed life.
You fill me, coating my wounds with Your Spirit;
"He is with me," spreads as a balm throughout my body.
I pray forgiveness, O God.
I had hoped, but not believed You would come;
Bringing the message I longed for: "He is with me."
For now I know, he is not far from me if You are in my heart.

—*Barbara Bruce Brakey*

• ▣ •

Where are you, O God? When the person I loved needed you most, where were you? When I need you most, where are you? There are so many questions, so few answers. My heart is aching, breaking, hurting and I cannot feel you with me. Reach out and grab hold of me so that I do not drown in my own tears. Help me to know that you have not abandoned me because I cannot take another loss. Where are you, O God? Hear my cry. Hear it now.

—*Mary Beth Hartenstein*

• ▣ •

Sharyl Peterson offers insight from her personal experience. "My mother died after a long struggle with Alzheimer's disease. My dad cared for her at home with incredible devotion and love, with my sister and me helping him as we could. Although it has been four-plus years since her initial diagnosis, I can still remember viscerally the utter terror and despair that gripped us all, a terror I experienced again when my husband developed some medical problems that led us to believe he too might be developing dementia. The following two prayers I've written for and used with parishioners who are themselves facing the devastation of a diagnosis of dementia":

Holy God, please hold _____ in this time of terror.
You know his/her/their anguish;
grant them strength to endure this moment, and then the next, and the next
one after that.
Fill their hearts, their spirits, their bodies
with the certain knowing
that whatever is to come,
You will be there with them, helping them through it. Amen.

O Lord –
　　right now, hope feels impossible.
So we ask instead
　　for strength of heart and of spirit,
and we ask that You hold our hands
　　as we walk forward
　　　　into what we cannot know. Amen.

—*Sharyl B. Peterson*

•■■•

"In terms of process, and practice, this was written using the practice of praying for the same person over several days—in this case, my colleague, who is retiring this year." Vince Amlin's insight is both about time and prayer and about the issue—retirement—itself a concern about both time and its meaning. "I challenged myself to focus on some different aspect of her transition each day. One day I prayed in thanksgiving for her many gifts. On another, I prayed about the challenges of loss of identity and purpose that can accompany retirement. I prayed another day for her children and grandchildren and what retirement would mean for them; and on another asking

God to deepen and enrich her marriage with the additional time she would have. I believe it was this multifaceted exploration (as well as the challenge to be brief) that led me to a more imagistic and metaphorical prayer. It seemed impossible to capture the breadth of my prayer for her in straightforward prose without going on for pages.

I saw that images of music kept popping up in my prayers: rhythm and rest. My colleague is also a wonderful dancer, who takes great joy in movement and choreography, so the prayer began to take shape around images of dance. Using figure and metaphor, I was able to say more with fewer words."

PRAYER FOR ONE HANGING UP HER DANCING SHOES

Time-keeping God,
as the hustling eighth notes
of working life stretch
and slow to a gentler rhythm,
grant your servant
whole notes of rest.

Then put on some
samba or rumba,
something syncopated
to make her smile,
and swing her hips,
and shake off
the specter of seriousness.

And finally,
when knees and ankles
are no longer
on speaking terms,
give her pleasure in simply swaying,
joy in watching
the little ones
jump up and
join the dance.

—*Vince Amlin*

PRAYER FOR RETIREMENT

God, so powerful
I wonder if you understand me—
after all, my children are older than Jesus.

I am afraid of being erased by retirement.

I am afraid of senior discounts
and feeling discounted,
of social security that means
social insignificance,

of knowing in my heart
that when people ask, "what do you do?"
all the things I do
are not what they are asking.

Help me feel my way into
being an elder,
Anna and Nicodemus,
bold prophet and still-seeking,
born again
into honoring my age
and not being its victim. Amen.

—Maren Tirabassi

FOR A PERSON FACING OLD AGE

Who have I become?
Steps unsure, eyes blurred, thoughts jumbled and slow,
but I am your child.
Hold this new me close, O God.

—Jerry Hebenstreit

• ◧◧ •

A PRAYER FROM A SUMMER STILL LIFE, JOSEPHINE AND KOI

God who wakes goldfish from pond mud and settles on her usual bench
a ninety-eight-year-old woman without teeth who feeds them a hot dog bun,
warm these your children with the deeper gold of August sun,
and shine indiscriminately even on others so discontented
they don't now remember the summer taste and feel of peace. Amen.

—*Maren Tirabassi*

• ◧◧ •

Although there are many aspects of life that bring us anxiety, frustration, and fear because we cannot control them or stop them from becoming a part of who we are, we also have much to rejoice over. Yes, today we may be old, but we are also wise! One day, we may be sick, but another, we give thanks on our knees for our good health. We may be lonely, or grieving, or struggling, but in the whole of the world, many prayers are being lifted up on our behalf!

We are grace seekers. We are grace givers. We are openhearted, dancing-in-God's-word people, and for all the moments we have been given, let us take time to give thanks. Kipp shares his perspective on this:

"The idea that gave birth to this transformed into conscious prayer my participation in a favorite hobby: home brewing. There are monasteries that have supported themselves for centuries through the brewing of beer, and Martin Luther is said to have utilized the caloric content of strong beer to sustain himself during lengthy fasts. If Jesus turned water into wine, then perhaps there are intrinsic spiritual possibilities in the transformation of barley, hops, water, and yeast into beer, though the alchemy is different.

It is not only the thaumaturgy that differs between home brewing and the miracle at Cana, however. The home brewer's final key ingredient is time. The initial outlay involves preparing the pot and other equipment, and giving a few hours over to steeping, boiling, transferring the mix into the fermenter. All must be done with care and attention. After the yeast is added comes the waiting. It may take a couple of weeks for the yeast to do its job, working through the grainy water to digest the extra sugars and morph into beer. Over this time, providing that it has been properly sealed and attended to, it may be forgotten about—but it does not stop working. Thus has a hobbyist's endeavor become a metaphor for the movement of the Spirit: with proper tending and care, something bracing comes forth that is ultimately beyond the brewer's ability to entirely control. And, as with the end product of home brewing, the best part lies in the sharing."

A HOME BREWER'S PRAYER

Wild and yeasty God, you who image your realm in a lump of leaven, let your spirit work its fermentation within me. Grant me the grace to pay proper attention, to undertake the labors that help lay the conditions that make possible your invisible work. And as my brews usually do, God, surprise me with the unpredictable directions of your leavening, the transmutation of good into good, of work into delight, of life into sharing. Amen.

—*Kipp Gilmore-Clough*

• 🎲 •

God, surprise us all with the unpredictable directions of your leavening, the transmutation of good into good, of work into delight, of life into sharing.
    Amen.

3

VINTAGE WINE IN VINTAGE WINESKINS, UNCORKED

Traditional Liturgy

When Jerry Hebenstreit reflects about preparing traditional worship, he says, "I still spend a good deal of time letting scriptures rattle around in my head to see what they say to me. And I try to get a sense of where the congregation is so I can connect to that, too. So I think about individuals in situations and what prayers they might want/need to hear, replaying scripture again and again."

Just because this is a chapter on traditional worship, or perhaps because it is traditional worship, it is important to invite the prayer-writing into new and writing-on-the-heart kinds of ways, like Jerry listening to an imaginary iPod playing the Sunday lectionary.

To remind us that writing traditional liturgy is a very contemporary gift, some suggestions for spiritual practices to inspire prayer-writing will be embedded in this chapter, and called "a writing moment now." "A writing moment now" is something to try, perhaps a new thought to inhabit but always a hand to the pencil, to the keys.

A writing moment now may be letting a line of scripture surprise us by reducing it to a tweet or expanding it like a mash-up novel, writing it in the sand at the beach or on a post-it note on the window through which we see the world! To whom could we text this? How hard would it be to memorize it? Once the scripture is integrated into life and the congregation is fully in the heart's eye, fresh liturgical writing can begin.

CALL TO WORSHIP, FROM LUKE 15

One: Our God comes running out to meet us
like a joyful old father on spindly legs—

**Many: He doesn't care that he looks the fool for us;
we are welcomed home with giddy gladness.**

One: Our God opens arms wide to embrace us
like an indulgent mother, even when we are resentful of one another—

**Many: She doesn't hold our jealousy against us;
we are welcomed into the celebration even then.**

One: Our God invites us to be more like a foolish, indulgent, loving parent—

**Many: We are welcomed to share in God's prodigal love for all:
love even for those who frustrate us,
love even for ourselves.**

All: Let us willingly enter the celebration.

—Sharon Benton

OPENING PRAYER, FROM PSALM 133

One: Behold, God's beloved, how good it is this morning

Many: that God's people come together to worship in unity.

One: It is like a refreshing rain in the torrid heat of summer

Many: washing over us and cleansing our spirits.

One: For God's blessing has been ordained in this place.

Many: We shall have life forevermore!

—Jerry Hebenstreit

• ♦♦ •

DOXOLOGY, ORDINARY TIMES

Praise God, who fills our lives with song,
Praise God, who has us sing along,
Praise God, whose music fills the air,
Praise God, who calls us all to care.

—*John H. Danner*

• ♦♦ •

"It's not possible for me to think of a Call to Worship or Morning Prayer apart from the rest of a worship service," Abigail Hastings writes. "I think of the Call as the transition from the disparate worlds we have come from and the one we enter together woven with threads of the themes of the coming hour. The Morning Prayer continues that idea—and, often to reinforce that feeling, phrases from music or readings find their way into the call or prayer."

We come from disparate worlds, and, sometimes, desperate ones. The transitional moments at the very beginning of worship form a bridge into a community. We take great care in shaping this time because it is in these moments that many decide if they will cross over into worship or simply sit for a while and return the way they have come. (Of course, such sitting—sometimes all that a person can manage—is itself not a bad thing!)

CALL TO WORSHIP, FROM PSALM 100

One: Make a joyful noise, all the earth! Come before God singing!

Many: Singing like leaves in a breeze. Singing like rain on a hot road. Singing like uncontrollable sneezes.

One: Enter into worship with thanksgiving and praise!

Many: Thanksgiving for a place to give thanks among others. Praise for the abundance of God's blessings.

One: For God is good. And God's love lasts longer than anything!

All: So make a joyful noise all people, all nations, all creation!
Make a joyful noise, all the earth!

—*Sharon Benton*

• 🎲 •

We come to worship from many different cultures. These gathering words from Canadian First Nations people lift up images unique to that culture—the tree and the hoop. These images of our "setting," of the place in which we sit down, do not divide us. They enrich us. Worship is not a choice between scriptural symbols or cultural metaphors—both are lively and inviting.

A writing moment now might invite us to write a call to worship informed by the very particularity of culture, engaged not by a concept or a season or a section of the service but by an image . . .

GATHERING OURSELVES FOR WORSHIP

One: In the centre stands a tree, encompassed by a hoop.

Many: What is the significance of this symbol?

One: The tree stands for our spirituality, ever reaching upward.

Many: What then of the hoop; what does it mean?

One: The hoop is our community of faith, ever stretching outward.

Many: Are there more teachings contained here?

One: The tree can grow because it is rooted in the faith of our ancestors.

Many: So what about the hoop; can it grow as well?

One: Indeed it will, so long as we are open to renewal and inclusive of difference.

Many: Let us celebrate the potential for growth in our spirituality and community of faith.

—*R. Matthew Stevens*

• 🎲 •

We name ourselves in worship, as well as those who come and are in community with us. We don't need to do so. We recognize that God's hospitality embraces us all, and yet we each know how important it is when someone remembers our "names." Lindsay Popper's lists in the following Call to Worship make the wide invitation so real.

A writing moment now would be to reflect on our own list of who it is who comes to worship . . . "we have . . ." "we bring . . ." "we are . . ." and then re-write Lindsay's prayer using those lists for the "many" part. Perhaps a different prayer will be called forth. Perhaps at this moment it will not. Writing down the list is, however, the beginning of intercession.

CALL TO WORSHIP

One: God, we come to you from different places.

Many: We have birthed children, lost jobs, fallen in love, wrestled with our fears, packed our bags. We have come looking for you, and your Spirit meets us, welcoming us just as we are.

One: God, we come to you bringing different things.

Many: We bring our questions, doubts, joys, suspicions, and gifts. We have come needing you in diverse ways, and your Spirit meets us, welcoming us just as we are.

One: God, we have come to you as different people.

Many: We are lawyers, parents, students, musicians, Star Trek aficionados, and baby-bird foster-fathers. We bring our whole selves to this place, and your Spirit meets us, welcoming us just as we are.

—*Lindsay Ruth Popper*

PRAYER OF CONFESSION

Almighty God, help us to see ourselves as You see us.
We pray to You for blessings, but rarely reach out to the poor.
We cry to You for safety, but stand mute in the face of oppression and injustice.

We call to You for peace, but take no steps to end war and violence.
Help us to see how far we are from where You call us to be.
Forgive our blindness, O God.

Assurance of Grace

God heals the retinas of the spirit so that we understand the hopes and sufferings of others. Secular culture calls this "empathy." We recognize it as "forgiveness," a wonderful and uncomfortable blessing.

—Jerry Hebenstreit

In the vintage worship services held in the beautiful wineskins of paper or electronic bulletins, there are not only liturgies used on many Sundays, but also those that are written for specific liturgical seasons and biblically based holy days, as well as some written for other holy days such as Reformation Sunday, All Saints Day, and World Communion Sunday. In the autumn, we also have the ancient celebration of Thanksgiving, which is assigned to different days in different countries. These occasions invite the shaping of worship into connected and thematic pieces. The obvious danger is to simply deposit these services into the calendar annually without always rethinking and repraying what their themes uniquely mean each year.

(Thanksgiving in Canada comes early in October.)

THANKSGIVING CALL TO WORSHIP

One: From the eagles' aerie, to the fishes' deep—

Many: from the colour-drenched leaves, to the rain-drenched street
(or *"to the frost-covered street"—the first is Vancouver, the second is just about everywhere else!*)

One: with our lips, with our hearts, with our hands, with our feet—

Many: we sing out, "ALLELUIA!"
we laugh out, "HOSANNA!"
we shout out, "THANK YOU, LOVING GOD!"
One: For all that was.

Many: **For all that is.**

One: For all that will be.

Many: **Alleluia. Hosanna! THANK YOU, LOVING GOD!**

One: For all that we were.

Many: **For all that we are.**

One: For all that we could be!

Many: **Alleluia. Hosanna! THANK YOU, LOVING GOD!**

One: So, together we sing . . .

Many: **Let it be.**

One: Together we say . . .

Many: **May it always be so.**

One: Together we shout . . .

All: **AMEN!**

—Richard Bott

•••

WORLD COMMUNION LITANY

Our congregation is truly multicultural. We have members from Nigeria, Cameroon, the Philippines, Jamaica, San Martin, as well as African—and European-Americans. During the procession of the breads, we have four people from the four corners of the globe carry four styles of bread to the table:

Procession of the Breads

One: From the four corners of the world, we praise God for the bread of life.

Many: **From Asia and the Pacific Rim, we bless God for the abundance of faith with which our brothers and sisters in Christ inspire us.**

One: Lord, we accept this blessing of sustenance.

Many: **From Africa and Australia, we thank God for the challenges of mission and of accepting our differences that our sisters and brothers in Christ seek to share with us.**

One: Lord, we accept this gift of understanding.

Many: From Europe and the lands to the glacial north, we ask God for strength to accept our history and learn from our brothers and sisters in Christ who have taught us in faith.

One: Lord, we accept this gift of knowing.

Many: From Central and South America and the many islands of the Caribbean, we seek to share the joy of laughter and music and patience that our sisters and brothers in Christ have given us in humility.

One: Lord, we accept this gift of worship.

Words of Institution, 1 Corinthians 11:23–26

Pastor: Our good news in Christ is this:

We are the children of God, seeking a touch of love and blessing from Christ. We are invited to take a place of honor at the table of the Lord. We come to this table, not because we are distinguished and important among humankind, but because we come humbly and gratefully.

Beloved, the table is set. We are invited to dine.

The Lord Jesus on the night when he was betrayed took a loaf of bread, and when he had given thanks, he broke it and said, "This is my body that is for you. Do this in remembrance of me."

In the same way he took the cup also, after supper, saying, "This cup is the new covenant in my blood. Do this, as often as you drink it, in remembrance of me."

For as often as you eat this bread and drink the cup, you proclaim the Lord's death until he comes.

—*LL Kroouze DuBreuil*

LL Kroouze DuBreuil, who wrote the preceeding World Communion Liturgy, says of all her worship preparation, "I look at the context of the congregation—spiritually, physically, theologically. Then I look into my heart to find what I also need to hear and say." This happens as well in Sharon Benton's prayer for Reformation Sunday and then the Totenfest prayer that follows.

REFORMATION SUNDAY

O Holy Spirit—we are creatures shaped by nature and nurture.
We inherit our ancestors' genetic codes:
a grandfather's uniquely copper-tinted hair,
a great aunt's dynamic speaking voice,
countless consistencies we may never realize
have gone before and will come again.
And we grow into ourselves under culture's bias:
learning desires and dreams unique to
this particular generation,
this land of expectation.
We are creatures formed by nature and nurture.

Yet you, O Spirit, are ever mutable,
always forming and re-forming,
shaping us anew from the stuff we have been.

You, O Spirit, are the gentle caress
that can re-form our hearts after they have been
bruised by hurtful relationship, loss of hope, or sorrow.
You are the fiery passion
that can re-form our actions,
embolden us to live outside Western expectations
of comfort and ease and indifference.
You are the ever-present stirring
that sharpens our minds,
instilling within us the longing to re-form our thoughts
and reach new conclusions about this world, faith, neighbor, and self.

You, O Spirit, are the wind that seizes
the edges of our own spirits,
inspiring us to ever re-form who we think we are—
as individuals, and as Christ's church.

Re-form us now, O Spirit, and in every moment,
to truly do your work and be your people.

In the spirit of One who lived his life in constant reformation, amen.

—*Sharon Benton*

••••

TOTENFEST/ALL SOULS DAY

God of Love,
you feel our loss when we remember
loved ones no longer with us in this life.
And you feel our longing when memories
like photographs
slide through our minds with startling clarity.
And you feel like wrapping your love around us
just as we feel like wrapping our arms around
our loved ones again.

God of Love,
slip peace quietly into the spaces where these holes hide in us:
peace where grief has grown,
peace where fear of the future has framed our imaginings,
peace where anger has bit into us with each sharp
"why?" or "how?" or "what now?"

Fill our holes—each and all of us who experience
pain or disease or addiction or need of any kind—
fill our holes with your undying love.

Fill us so we may know that life continues through your Spirit—
here and now,
and eternally.

—*Sharon Benton*

•••

We write liturgy for the people who are gathered in our pews, flexible seating, flash churches, or virtual congregations. We try to understand who they are and what their longings are. We also need to write liturgy for these insiders that reminds them that many are left out. We name those excluded from our hearts—cheaters, scammers, felons, those with a radically different political or theological understanding. Who are the hardest to love . . . insider traders, pedophiles?

LITANY

All: We are the body of Christ!
Let us be your eyes in the world—

Men: To see the needs of your people

Women: To notice the pain and suffering

All: And not close our eyes!
Let us be your ears in the world—

Women: To hear the cries for help from those who cannot help themselves

Men: To listen to those who feel they have no voice

All: And hear the Christ within them calling to us to care.
Let us be your hands in the world—

Men: To do the work of caring, for our loved ones,
for the neighbor, for those who cannot work

Women: To work alongside those who are struggling

All: And know the joy of community.
Let us be your arms in the world—

Men: To give the shoulder for support

Women: To give a needed hug

All: And to know you are there for them, for all of us.
Let us be your feet in the world—

Women: To walk the mile when there is need

Men: To share the load

All: And to know the burden is light with you
We are the body of Christ!
We will strive to be your presence in this world. Amen.

—*Devoree Clifton Crist*

• 🔲 •

CONFESSIONAL PRAYER FOR HEALING OF BROKENNESS

Grace-filled God, our fears, doubts, worries, and obsessions can be such giants in our lives. They seem so much bigger than we are. We lose faith in our ability to overcome these giants with your love. So much seems wrong in the world; we're unsure if we have enough of our goodness to change it. Storms of sin and temptation batter at us: cynicism, hatred, self-indulgence, numbness, and hopelessness. Forgive us, God. Remind us to open our hearts so you can heal us, to listen to your words of peace and joy. As we open our lives to you, we become the confident, beloved servants of your holy, ever-creating purpose.

Assurance of Grace

God has so much grace and blessing for us and only asks that we choose it. Choose it—let God forgive you.

—*Alan F. Parker*

• 🔲 •

OFFERING DEDICATION

Beckoning God, we are tempted to leave the work of justice to police officers and judges, the work of care to nurses and therapists, the work of spiritual matters to clergy. But you call to all of us to give of ourselves: our energy, our resources, our skills, as we are able and as we are needed. We dedicate these gifts and our whole lives in order to share and fulfill the work of justice and care, ever rooted in an awareness of your presence. Amen.

—*Jeff Nelson*

•••

We pause between a prayer of dedication and a thanksgiving prayer—one that is so specific to the Thanksgiving holiday in the United States that it mentions the odd occasion commonly called Black Friday that follows the Thursday holiday and features middle-of-the-night sales by retailers to encourage Christmas present shopping. Both the weekly prayer of dedication and the annual occasion of Thanksgiving invite us to explore gratitude.

In this time and place, we consider gratitude. We are grateful to other people—those who do the work of justice. We are grateful for the responsibility to dedicate our own gifts. We are grateful for grace moments that season even the intervals in our lives that mostly taste like tears. Those are notes that Jeff Nelson and Sharon Benton strike.

A writing moment now would be to explore the particularity of gratitude . . . maybe as a list, maybe as wordless contemplation . . . and allow that to unfold in prayer.

THANKSGIVING

Sometimes gratitude comes hard, O Spirit:
hard as bricks thrown through a stained-glass Jesus feeding his flock;
hard as teeth grinding their own enamel night after anxious night;
hard as fighting through Black Friday shopping crowds.
Sometimes gratitude comes hard, O Spirit:
when there is loss of relationship,
loss of abilities,

loss of life,
loss of hope.

But then a wet nose nuzzles us awake in the morning,
or a stranger captures our wind-stolen scarf,
or a single star stretched out in so much space reminds us—
 we are not alone in this life:
 we are one with each creature,
 and with each other,
and with each part of your creation.

Spirit, our individual griefs are not small,
nor are the world's pains.
But grant us gratitude amidst them
so we may also overcome
 addiction, depression, disease, or accident;
 poverty and war and all that depletes life rather than sustains it.

Even when gratitude is hard, O Spirit,
soften us to see your love poured out upon all the universe,
and help us give thanks.

—*Sharon Benton*

• •• •

Beverley Osborn begins with a list, but then invites a contemplation, resisting the prayer-writer's desire to save God time by choosing prayer results like the contents of a spiritual shopping cart in an online order. She says:

"When I'm preparing intercessory prayer I usually go for categories of people, for example, refugees, prisoners, people who work in the night; then I invite the congregation to hold these folk before God in love. I always offer a silent space for them to do this. At the end I pray that God will transform the prayers and love we have offered into the words and works and people that will help or heal or make a positive difference."

AFFIRMATIONS OF FAITH

We believe in a God who cares deeply about all people.
We believe in a God who has come into our lives and our hearts.
We believe in a God who has given us the work
of showing God's unconditional love and extravagant welcome to all people.
We believe in a God who walks beside us.
We believe there is nowhere our God will not go,
and so we see our God everywhere:
in the faces of men sitting on park benches or driving city buses,
in babies in strollers and elders in wheelchairs.
We see our God holding the hands of women walking into abortion clinics,
sitting in our congresses and parliaments.
We see our God working the night shift with factory workers,
walking the streets beside sex workers,
waking up early with those who make our breakfast,
walking the halls beside bullied middle schoolers,
crossing the desert with people looking for a chance at a better life.
Our God sits beside us in prison cells, delivery rooms, police cars,
corner offices, fast-food cash registers, and tractors.
We see our God in all people,
and we pray that we let our lives show God's love in us.

—*Lindsay Ruth Popper*

"It dawned on me one night as I lay in bed mulling over some of the prayers I had written . . . there is more often another stage in my process these days," Jerry Hebenstreit reflects. "It's a desire to take thoughts from 'nice' (or whatever word I really mean) to something approaching 'beautiful.' So many times the basic idea feels good, but there is a hint of another level that can reach deeper into the heart. An image isn't quite right or a phrase is understandable but lacks something indefinable. I hope that doesn't sound too precocious or aesthetic."

The thin tinsel of the season that stretches from Advent to Epiphany is so often about beauty. When worship words truly name the hopes and fears of all the year that rest in this time and the Bethlehem memory, they are beautiful—even when they draw tears. When they are shallower than beauty they become "cute" and when they are deeper than beauty they stumble into silence.

DOXOLOGY, ADVENT

Praise God who calms our ev'ry fear,
Who holds us close and counts us dear,
Who gives us hope when nights grow long,
And fills our hearts with grateful song.

—John H. Danner

•🎞•

DOXOLOGY, CHRISTMAS

Praise God with joyful heart and mind,
For in the manger we will find,
The One who gives us hope and peace,
The One in whom our troubles cease.

—John H. Danner

•🎞•

Almost too familiar, the Matthew 1 and Luke 2 scriptures, a one-two punch of Christmas Eve, are supposed to knock us out. As liturgical planners we assume they are familiar—that memories of childhood candles burning will entrance us into the holiness. It isn't enough. Many of the people in our churches don't have the memories to access either the scriptures themselves or the candlelight and "Silent Night." They need the words fresh and new. They are desperate for a liturgy that engages them in the story.

CHRISTMAS

One: You come to us with womb-wrinkled skin and thirsty, searching lips.

Many: We offer to you our own vulnerability.

One: You come to us on a bed of straw where sheep have lain and cows have fed.

Many: We offer to you our own humility.

One: You come to us with loving purpose in your bones and justice on your breath.

Many: We offer to you our own wills.

One: Blessed Baby, Compelling Prophet, you come to us again in this moment, and in every moment without end.

Many: In thanks and praise, we offer the whole of our lives to you.

—*Sonja Ingebritsen*

• ◍ •

Abigail Hastings is the ultimate lover of Calls to Worship and Opening Prayers. They are so much more than a liturgical clearing of the throat, the throwaway before the real deal begins. They are the Call! It's shofar time, folks! Is there anything more presumptuous, hopeful, crazy, and prodigal-Mama in all the world than inviting people to be in worship together?

So, for Abigail, an opening prayer for New Year is the opposite of the sad-tinsel-time it can be for many of us. She writes about the artistic inspiration for her prayer that follows. "This service included special music by the legendary performer Jomama Jones (Daniel Alexander Jones), who co-wrote with Bobby Halvorson a powerful song called 'Open.' It includes the line 'If your world falls apart, rearrange the broken pieces' and repeats the refrain 'Give yourself to save yourself.' So the reference in the prayer echoes what had just been heard to keep those wonderful phrases in hearts and minds."

A PRAYER FOR THE NEW YEAR

O God, in whom we live and move and have our being,
we begin a new dance with you again today.

We mark our days in arbitrary ways—it must seem so funny—
but on this new day in this new year
we confess to being so bold
as to ask that we might be co-creators with you.

Help us, O God, that we too may create beauty out of nothingness;
help us envision elegant solutions to intractable problems,
to manufacture usefulness and purpose and intention
that in this new year we might surprise ourselves
    with what we can accomplish together.

Create in each of us a clean heart, O God. Give us
new eyes to see the needs of others, renewed energy
for the work to be done, and in so doing,
    to spread joyfulness in the pleasure of living.

Create in us a new idea about ourselves, that we might find mercy
and forgiveness within, and cast aside impediments
to being most fully who we are meant to be.
Rearrange the broken pieces.
Teach us how to give ourselves to save ourselves.

O God, we thank you for this community of people, for the commitment to
reach those who need a cool cup of water in whatever form that may take.
Bless us now as we reimagine and expand the reach of our fountain, a fountain drawn from the source of life and love, ever flowing into our days. Amen.

—*Abigail Hastings*

• ◦◦ •

Abigail also notes this about her piece. "More than a hundred years ago our church
provided an actual water fountain, sorely needed, to those living in nearby tene-
ments of the day—and that was the tie-in to the concluding line." This church really
knew how to make a big splash with their giving!

Prayers of dedication for Morning Offering are also not "throwaways." In sub-Saharan Africa, worshipers often dance forward their gifts and offerings after having exchanged bills to the very smallest denomination—so they can dance past the plate more often! "Give away," not "throw away," is so much fun.

Often we don't have fun during the offertory. Maybe we give too little. Maybe we feel awkward talking about money in church. Maybe passing the plate feels too ritualistic when more contributions to ministry and mission come by direct deposit.

PRAYER OF DEDICATION

O God of the Real Thing, we come before you with our true selves, not looking for a good deal or a quick fix. Help us to share your love with others through our gifts today and our whole lives, not because there's a bonus buy in it for us but because everyone is in the market for your good news. Amen.

—*Sonja Ingebritsen*

• ▦ •

The season of Epiphany is the season of revelation. The traditional texts flow from Magi visit to Jordan baptism, then split into three tributaries of the ways human beings come to know God, finally converging in the Transfiguration. It is so much more than the time-of-carols-fading between the drama of Advent and Lent. These are important scriptures.

Amy Sens says, "This week I sat down to finish things up and did my usual meditation, which is to write the scripture out by hand. I wrote the two verses at the top of each page as I was revising one of the prayers, writing out several versions of it. When I preach I do something similar, copying out the Bible reading by hand before working on the sermon."

A writing moment now would be simply to write out a verse. One may be in mind because of personal issues, or because it might be involved in worship soon. One way to do this would be to write the scripture on lined paper, leaving alternate lines blank, and putting personal thoughts that emerge in the empty lines.

STEWARDING OUR STORIES

You have given us your Word, O God, and we think we can keep your Word bound in a dusty book, safe and harmless. But you are a God who will not be bound, a God who breaks all binding. Break our bondage to what we have learned of your word, Holy One. Open us to relationship with the stories of those who have gone before us. Open us to encounter your Word anew. Amen.

—Sharon Benton

INVOCATION

O God, surround us with your love, envelop us in your grace, clothe us with your compassion. Send forth your spirit so we may hear your word and internalize it for our lives. We come before you as open vessels ready to be filled.

—Devoree Clifton Crist

PRAYER OF CONFESSION

Almighty God,
You tell us what You want of us . . .
do what is right,
speak only what is true,
do no evil to our neighbors.
Yet time after time we stumble and fall.
We step back from the right thing because it's too risky.
We tell small lies to make ourselves look good.
We harm our neighbors as payback for real or imagined slights.
Forgive us, O God,
and patiently lead us back to Your ways and Your truth.

Assurance of Pardon:

One: Brothers and sisters, our God shows us the way.
Our God welcomes us back to the truth.
Our God stands at the center of our lives.
Our God forgives us.

Many: Thank You, O God,
for Your boundless love,
for Your unending patience,
for Your overflowing mercy.
Glory be to the God who forgives and restores.

—*Jerry Hebenstreit*

• ▓ •

Epiphany is the season of knowing and growing, but it is hardly a dull time—think of that trajectory from frankincense to glowing faces! Simone Weil once wrote of it, "Absolutely unmixed attention is prayer." We sometimes need epiphanies in order to direct our attention. Sometimes our worship should have an epiphany style as well as content—a little flash, a startle of spirit.

They are building a new bridge from the state of New Hampshire to the state of Maine—a drawbridge that will go up and down for ocean-going vessels. The morning newspaper carries a debate about whether the bridge should be illuminated and, if so, who should pay for it. In church Sunday terms, Epiphany is the bridge between Christmas and Lent, and in theological terms, it is the illumination between them.

Gracious, patient God, we live so much less than you hope for us. We reside in fear, and we teach fear to our children. Our fear steals life from us and from the world. Help us to know anew how sweet and holy your creation is; how its promise is for all, for those we do not know, even for those we fear and scorn. Help us to look for beauty, not for brokenness. Help us to look for life, not death. Help us to sing to the world of that life and beauty and, in so doing, shower it on the broken places in our hearts and in the darkest corners of your world of promise . . .

—*Alan F. Parker*

• 👀 •

If Simone Weil's insight is more contemplative, Lindsay Popper moves from the passive to the active. "Writing, to me," she says, "is a way of staying connected to the world, and I see paying attention as a central act of worship."

We pay attention. We pray attention. We pray nature into the sanctuary. If we are liturgists, we pray our personal week all around the pews and hope that its very specificity allows those who are sitting in them to celebrate the precious ordinary details of their own lives. R. Matthew Stevens gathers people to worship in Epiphany in his Canadian First Nations community, and he begins with snow. In Australia and Argentina and Aotearoa the weather is late summer. Barbara Murray from Aotearoa, New Zealand, lifts up that truth. We read each, not to choose, but as Lindsay Popper says, to stay connected to the world.

GATHERING OURSELVES FOR WORSHIP

One: A snow-covered landscape, nearly barren except for a few trees, all shrouded in mist.

Many: We've all experienced winter this way, cold, dreary, and lonely.

One: Yet even in winter there are many simple pleasures to be found.

Many: A cup of hot chocolate after a brisk walk, a roaring fire in the hearth, a gathering of family or friends over a hearty meal.

One: And if we look closer, we'll see the first tentative sprigs of grass peeking up through the snow.

Many: The trees are not just any trees, but evergreens, perseverance against the cold and darkness, and eventual triumph over it.

One: Most significantly, these green symbols speak of persistent faith;

of a hope expressed amid the wintery landscape; of the joy of that hope's rebirth.

Many: A new world is being created, and if we place our hope in God's redemptive power, that new world is ours as well.

One: If your life has had too much of barrenness and cold, I welcome you into this place where today we celebrate the warmth of that new world.

Many: Let us all join in worshiping the Creator, who makes all things new!

—*R. Matthew Stevens*

• 👓 •

Creator God, We see your handiwork in the order of our world. In the infinite variety of plants and flowers and how they provide food for different animal and bird life. In the food chain of the oceans. In the changing seasons; from wet to dry in the tropics; from summer to autumn in New Zealand; from winter to spring in the northern hemisphere. We thank you for the rain we have had for our gardens and for the farms and orchards. We thank you for cooler temperatures at night.
Creator God, we thank you.

—*Barbara Murray*

• 👓 •

OFFERING PRAYER, OPEN AND AFFIRMING SUNDAY

Spirit of openness and affirmation, we dedicate these gifts to the ministry of love and acceptance in the world. May we ever seek to use all of our resources to create a world and a church where all are welcome and honored, loved and fully known. This we pray in the name of Jesus, who welcomed everyone to his table. Amen.

—*Sharon Benton*

• 👓 •

Earlier in this book we quoted Kathy Moore as suggesting that we would do well to have a little Lent in us all the time, so it makes sense to begin this season with her words.

"Many of my prayers are inspired by a particular person—in fact, by a person who has irritated me," she says. "It's easy to pray for the people who delight me and comfort me, and they are many. One of my prayers is for someone who seems to me lost in the mists of the new age and rather unable to see other people—me for example—through her preoccupation with her own spirituality. But then I thought—it could as easily be about me.

"Then I focused on scripture—Jeremiah 31:31–34 (writing on the heart); John 8:1–11 (especially verses 6–8, the holiness of dust-writing); John 20:30–31 (why we write any of it); John 21:24–25 (there are so many more stories!)":

Oh God, write on my heart as you have promised,
And if it hurts that tender, swollen part, give me strength.
Tell me the stories unwritten; let me tell the stories unwritten,
But quietly,
As you remind my patience, yet again, to write in the dust
until you have spoken
and I have drunk my fill.

—*Kathleen Moore*

•••

DOXOLOGY, FIRST SUNDAY IN LENT

Praise God, who gives us strength to bear,
The challenge found most ev'rywhere.
Praise God, who serves as friend and guide:
Temptation helps to set aside.

—*John H. Danner*

•••

God, your love is our shield, our roadmap, and our resting place. Put your love between our judgment and those who are different from us, between our lust and those who want only to be seen as human and whole, between our anger and the people who have let us down. Put your love between our apathy and the hurting world that needs our care, between our fatigue and the work you have for us to do, between our fears and the good life you have prepared for us. Your love is the only thing big enough to bridge all of the broken places in this world, so help us open our lives up fully to you, the God whose name is love.

—*Lindsay Ruth Popper*

• ◼ •

PRAYER OF DEDICATION

From the bones we scatter before you, make blessing. Clothe them with flesh, and breathe your Spirit into their lungs. Cause this new body of blessing to walk among your people everywhere, inviting life even in the desolate places. Amen.

—*Sonja Ingebritsen*

• ◼ •

Often the biblical text is engaged to inform a sermon. Mary Beth Hartenstein reads the text before writing the prayer or the service. There is a holy circle in moving from ancient text into human spirit into prayer through people to God again. She says:

"I take time to read and reflect on the text myself. After some time, I begin typing words and phrases that I want to use to capture what I think the Spirit is moving in me and through me. Writing my prayer becomes my prayer. I often simply sit at my computer and let the words flow from my heart and mind and spirit onto the page. I try to experiment with adjectives and adverbs to help paint a picture so that those listening to the words of the prayer can participate by seeing and experiencing the movement of what is offered."

Ken Sehested paints such a picture of the cousin of Jesus of Nazareth:

JOHN THE BAPTIZER

John. Such a tame name for a man born to inhabit the wild side of heaven's incursion into earth's contempt. You startle children with your leather-girdled, camel-haired attire, hot breath calling the devout into the

Jordan's penitential wake. What brings you and your honey-smeared beard into such a barren land?

Spirit-drenched baptizer of repentant flesh, exposing hearts to the advent of mercy, announcing dawn's infiltration of destiny's dark corner.

Witness to the Spirit-dove's descent, confirming Elizabeth's praise, Mary's assent, and Messiah's demand for the hills to bow and the valleys to heave.

Declaring the baptism of fire by the One to come, by refiner's flame fully pleasing to God and just as surely frightful to all who devise deceit and sponsor carnage.

The Baptizer's bargain is this: Enter these waters at the risk of all self-absorbed living. You've nothing to lose but frail fear.

A certain drowning is required for lungs to receive Breath from above on wings of a dove. There's no getting right with God. There's only getting soaked.

So wade in the water. Don't mind the mud. For God's gonna trouble that cleansing flood.

—*Kenneth L. Sehested*

• • •

Lent is a time of confession and assurance of grace. Sometimes we do this in worship like a call and response in a square dance with barely a pause for recognition, much less repentance. A writing moment now might begin with one of the familiar words of the season—fasting, repentance, reflection, temptation, ashes, prayer, justice, journey, Lent—and dwell with it, not jumping to preconceived notions or stereotypes, but following its path into a deeper experience. Introspection always turns outward. At that point it becomes liturgically rich; it's a prayer to carry not only one's own but also the deep experiences of others.

PRAYER OF FORGIVENESS AND CONFESSION

Forgiving and redirecting God, there are many times when confession seems an irrelevant and unnecessary exercise. We tell ourselves that we're basically good, certainly better than many whom we see featured in the news. When we come to this time of confession, our lists of glaring sins seem short; we feel affirmed more than repentant. Help us to take a second, deeper look at ourselves in order to identify not just actions we have committed, but those we have neglected. Help us to recognize attitudes of fear, selfishness, and prejudice that keep us from seeing you around us, especially in others whom you call your children. Refocus us toward your active and creative love for all creation and help us to embody it in all that we are and do. Amen.

—*Jeff Nelson*

• ▦ •

Loving God, we live in a land of winter.
Not the winter of the seasons, but the bleak winter of a life lived
    far from You.
Easter was so long ago. It has been hard to hold on to the joy
    of Resurrection
in the constant clamor and chatter of a dark world that can only
    be illuminated by
having more, having it now, having it loud, boisterous, colorful,
    unsatisfying.
What we truly need is Your light to shine bright among us once more.
Remind us again how You came to live among us,
    to share our humanity and
to show us how to truly live a life in Your love.
Come, O God, again to be among us. Your people wait in hope.

—*LL Kroouze DuBreuil*

• ▦ •

Lent also has these strange other times . . . Daylight Savings Time and April Fool's Day. And even the most traditional of traditional worship services needs a little blarney.

COLLECT FOR ST. PATRICK'S DAY

God, who makes a saint of Brigit
with a milk-miracle and a beer-miracle,
and who searches for even one lost snake
that's been driven out,
teach us Irish gifts—fiddling and potatoes,
storytelling and genuine wakes,
step-dancing, shamrocks,
and a good round blessing of ordinary things.

For we pray in this Trinity—
the lintel on the door, the peat in the hearth,
and the stranger who stands at the one,
in need of the other's warmth. Amen.

—*Maren Tirabassi*

COLLECT FOR DAYLIGHT SAVINGS TIME

God, awake before our first reluctant yawn,
help us treasure the spring beauty of daylight,
celebrate the savings in our lives,
and appreciate every moment
of every time,
so that we truly never lose an hour,
for we praise you with alarm,
with snooze button,
and—when we need it—
with a deep changing of all our clocks. Amen.

—*Maren Tirabassi*

BENEDICTION, APRIL FOOL'S DAY

May the blessing of God
—who turns the world upside-down—
be all around you.
May the blessing of a backwards Messiah
—who leads in all the wrong ways—
be within you.
May the blessing of a foolish Spirit
—who blows you to awkward and unexpected places—
open you to God's own mischief!

—*Sharon Benton*

Kipp Gilmore-Clough says, "I decided to begin by meditating on Psalm 139:14, 'I praise you, for I am fearfully and wonderfully made. Wonderful are your works; that I know very well.' So I sat with the verse, let my eyes play over it, my lips recite it, allowed it to turn over and over in my mind until my mind turned around it."

LITANY, FROM PSALM 139

One: You have searched me and know me.

**Many: Whatever I do, whatever I say,
you know me up and down, inside and out.**

One: There is no place I can be apart from you.

**Many: Wherever I go, near or far, good or bad, high or low, you are there.
I cannot hide from you even in the dark, for you are light in the darkness.**

One: For I am your creation, you have made me and care for me.

**Many: You knew me before I was born, and know me fully all my life,
all my ways, and love me.**

One: Save me from evil, O God.

Many: Look into my heart and help me be what you want me to be. Lead me on the right path.

—*Devoree Clifton Crist*

• ◾◾ •

SPRING FORWARD

Our spirits leap with the lengthening days, God of Seasons—
they strain forward into the hope
brought by damp, fertile earth
and neon greens beginning to temper winter's burn.

Our spirits leap with the hope spring brings:
new life, new opportunity for healing,
new rhythms to enter and explore.

Our spirits leap forward,
even as our Lenten journey
leads us closer to Jerusalem;
leads us to face the worst humanity can accomplish
by our unjust institutions and
unexamined cultural expectations,
leads us to look within, to see where
transformation must take place
if wholeness is to come.

As the light of our days grows longer, Bright Sun,
shine on us that we might see those places within
that need your transforming touch—your spring cleaning!
And shine your light on the places
where we might touch the world
and bring healing to it through our own shining lives.

—*Sharon Benton*

Holy Week is a powerful but potentially frustrating time in a congregation's worship life. For many, it means following Jesus' journey to Jerusalem through the gospels' words or through liturgical traditions—from stations of the cross to stations of justice, from Tenebrae shadowing to Good Friday fasts. Different worship leaders in different years make choices between a Palm or Passion Sunday focus. Some faith communities have deeply meaningful annual services of foot washing, Easter vigil, or sunrise service. Others choose different ritual opportunities each year. Traditions shift and change, seeking to serve the spiritual needs of a particular gathering of people.

Holy Week frustrations include the worry that too many people bounce from Hosanna to Alleluia with no opportunity to reflect on the themes of suffering and sacrifice. Other worship leaders feel internal or external "performance pressure" to share the resurrection through the richest music, most brilliant flowers and the wisest (yet most entertaining) of sermons. Letting that go is very hard. Richard Bott simplifies it all when he writes this:

"There is a practice that many of us who reflect on scripture in the midst of a congregation have. We say something like, 'May the words of our mouths and the meditations of our hearts be acceptable in your sight, O God, our strength and our redeemer.' It's those same words that come into my head every time I compose a prayer, a status update, or a tweet. There's something about taking just a minute or two to remind myself that being faithful is trying to ensure that everything I say (or type) is in line with how I understand God's love to be lived in the world."

PRAYER OF CONFESSION

One: God of our bodies, and God who met us through Jesus' body,

Many: Forgive us for spiritualizing you,
making you irrelevant to the tissues and tendons of life.
Forgive us for spiritualizing you,
forgetting Mary's birth pangs or your agony on the cross.
Forgive us for spiritualizing you,
dishonoring or neglecting our own bodies or the bodies of others.
Forgive us for spiritualizing you,

acting as single organisms when the truth is that we are a multi-organ body of creation.

Forgive us, and free us to live in our bodies for the sake of the One Body. Amen.

Assurance of Grace

One: For this freedom, God has created us. For this freedom, Christ has redeemed us. For this freedom, Spirit continues to guide us.

Many: **Thanks be to God.**

—*Sonja Ingebritsen*

BRIEF LITURGY FOR A HOLY WEEK SERVICE

Opening Prayer

God, someone's tipped-over-table entrepreneurial coin is rolling across the floor. This church could really use it. Yet we are a house of prayer. It's so shiny . . . but we have to let it go. Amen.

Dedication of Offering

Sometimes a gift just smells extravagant—baking bread, fresh laundry, funeral flowers, washed dog, nard from a broken alabaster jar. God, accept all our senses and whatever it is that reminds us of the scent of love. Help us always spend it. Amen.

Confession

God, we have cheated ourselves and you by puckering up for success and selfishness, for the secret words and deeds that hurt those dearest to us. Amen.

Assurance of Grace

Our forgiveness may not be enough to keep us from nodding off when love is confusing, but this grace we have—when someone pushes a bag of betrayal at us—we can say, "Kiss off."

Closing Prayer

We are a people of bunions because we do try to walk in the shoes of others. Our feet are not always pretty. Touch, us, Christ, and teach us the podiatry of love. Amen.

Benediction

Bless us with the old wisdom of olive trees,
the fresh taste of tears,
courage that looks at crowns and thorns,
and compassion that goes shopping for Sunday spice
to anoint those hurt by new crosses.

—Maren Tirabassi

• •• •

And then there is Easter—the Big Time, the Big Tent, the Big Bang that begins life all over again. Yet its big theology is hard to squeeze into the small packages of our worship services.

Christy Ackley Zuzelo says, "When I was writing these tweet-like prayers I was really struggling. Easter is a hard time for me, like it is for many people, and through thoughtful and prayerful reflection I started to understand why. I don't really remember Easter as a fun or comfortable time. My parents were both pastors, and I remember Easter as lots of expectations, lots of preparation, lots of busy-busy-busy for endless church services. Why is everyone so stressed out? Why is everyone so serious? Why am I so serious?

DOXOLOGY, EASTER

Praise God, who makes all those on earth,
Praise God, who grants all creatures worth,
Praise God, who gives us ev'ry breath,
And raises us to life from death.

—John H. Danner

LL Kroouze DuBreuil reminds us that "one of the joys of my call as a pastor is the writing of weekly liturgy and litanies for special occasions."

The most special of occasions, the holy day from which everything begins . . .

EASTER

From deep within our tombs we hear you call, O God:
Rise up!
Rise up from death into new life.

We have found new life in this spring season,
in children joyfully squirming among us,
in each deep breath we breathe.
We have found new life in people's struggle for
just government throughout the world,
and in nations' continued support
following natural disasters.

From deep within our tombs we hear you call, O God:
Rise up!
Rise up from death into new life.

We follow your voice in our hope to overcome
illness, grief, addiction, fear.
We follow your voice in our hope to heal your creation,
make whole our connection to all that is.

From deep within our tombs we hear you call, O God:
Rise up!
Rise up from death into new life.

Resurrecting God, you call to us to follow Christ,
to rise up from our tombs that hold us in death—
but you do not expect us to do so alone.

It is you who fill us with life beyond all our daily deaths.
It is you who strengthen us to bring life to others.

It is you, Holy One, whom we hear call within our tombs: rise up!

And so we do. We have. We are here. Amen.

—*Sharon Benton*

• ⬛ •

One: Easter resurrection is never as assured as the arrival of Easter bunnies.

Many: The Spirit rarely blows according to the calendar, much less on demand.

One: Yet we live with ears open, eyes peeled, hands and feet nimble.

Many: Ready for jolting news and a dash to one tomb or another.

One: This is the purpose of wakeful attention from Friday's crowed abandonment to Sunday's vernal dawn:

Many: Training in the art of vigilance. Watching. And waiting.

One: Nevertheless, one empty tomb is no threat to any Caesar's rule and reign.

Many: Any more than the annual and specially adorned sanctuary crowd on Easter morn.

One: The devil doesn't mind a packed church house.

Many: Clothiers and chocolate-makers yearn for the season as much as any cleric.

One: It's Easter's aftermath, of resurrection contagion, that threatens the seal of the tomb's dark terror.

Many: Ain't no grave can hold my body down!

—*Kenneth L. Sehested*

• ⬛ •

Christy Ackley Zuzelo found some answers for her questions. "Praying this week helped a lot. Praying for others, praying for myself, finding new ways to move forward, making Easter fun for my children, changing patterns, making new traditions, working to make sure all my obligations and responsibilities are helpful to me and my children and not hurtful. I want to love Easter, like I love Lenten transformations. I want my children to love Easter and the excitement and anticipation it brings, not expectations. I want to lighten up and have fun!"

In the contemporary worship chapter, we have several other funeral resources placed in the context of Holy Week before Easter. These selections, which are very personal, having been composed for specific individuals, seem to be a response to Easter itself and belong more appropriately after our celebration of the resurrection.

FUNERAL BLESSING

Dear _____, May the glory of the skies surround you and the light of sunlit waters be upon you. May the chuckle of laughing waves give joy to your journeying, the song of the tui accompany you and the strong wings of seabirds fly you into the freedom of eternal love.

And for those of us who are still earthbound, may the vitality of the fern be in our words and our ways, may the beauty of the earth renew our spirits, and may the tenderness of a new dawn bring us peace. Amen.

—*Beverley L. Osborn*

FUNERAL BLESSING

May the glory of coastal sunsets and the sparkle of wind-blown spray be upon you. May the music of the laughing river give you joy and the perfume of your garden flowers surround you. May the rhythm of the long waves be for you the pulse of the love that creates all life and goes beyond death. May the strong wings of the gulls fly you to your next adventure of the spirit.

And may we, your family and friends, go on our way with your generosity of work and spirit, your happy heart, and your energy and eagerness to live life to the full. Amen.

—*Beverley L. Osborn*

And then, as suddenly as it arrives, Easter is over, but our life of faith continues. As Ken Sehested says, "After the ecstasy comes the laundry . . ." There are also Good Shepherd Sunday and Earth Day and a cluster of secular holidays that culture attaches to the heartstrings.

One: Listen up, you heralds of hope: Hear the cheer of angels for your big, bold, even brassy acts of courage. Don't back down from the chance to be audacious, bodacious, maybe even contentious.

Many: But it is the tenacious on whom the Beloved most depends.

One: Quotidian faithfulness—in life's persistent, unremarkable moments, when no bands play, no cameras roll, no headlines appear—this is the persevering labor, which Redemption most employs. Ordinary time rocks.

Many: Remember these things, and teach your children well:
After the ecstasy comes the laundry.

One: Vision for mission begins with the street signs in your own neighborhood.

Many: The bonds you restore outweigh the bounty you confer.

One: An inch of fertile soil takes a millennium to amass. Plant sequoias and fruit trees whose yield you will not taste.

Many: Small stuff matters. An ounce of care is worth a ton of theory.

One: Foster the habits of daily attention and timely words to encourage.

Many: God's in the details; the devil prefers abstraction.

One: Come mothers and shepherds, gardeners and menders. Come fathers and healers, instructors, defenders.

Many: The rendezvous, of Heaven with earth, is announced with each pardon's release.

—*Kenneth L. Sehested*

GATHERING PRAYER, SPRINGTIME

Slowly, slowly the days grow longer;
Spring's iridescent glow overtakes winter's dim gloom.
Slowly, slowly our vision clears;
Light breaks down our darkness.
Come, let us approach the Light together;
Come, let us follow with the Shepherd who loves us!

—*Jerry Hebenstreit*

One: Well my friends, the time has come for us to quit this place of contemplation and reflection.

Many: We're so warm and comfy now, we've no desire to return to the bitter cold.

One: My friends, it is summer time now.

Many: It's not the weather that chills us through and through, but the cold indifference and bitter realities of daily life.

One: My brothers and sisters, the warmth we find here in Christian community can be easily carried away with each of us.

Many: In the week ahead may I not only be sustained by the love of God, but may I also share it as graciously as I received. Amen.

—*R. Matthew Stevens*

Earth Day, or Integrity of Creation Sunday, is an unusual observance in some churches. It celebrates the natural world and urges advocacy on its behalf on a particular day, even though many communities of faith consider these issues perennial. However, in those congregations for whom care of the earth is not named and claimed often, a Sunday in Eastertide can be chosen to place joy and grief, hope and fear for the earth and its future in the minds of worshipers.

TALK WITH THE EARTH, AND SHE WILL TEACH YOU, JOB 12:8A

Halt. Stop yourself and listen.
Observe, appreciate,
breathe, dance, laugh, cry,
enjoy your freedom,
enjoy the beauty
of everything that surrounds you.

Halt. Stop yourself and look,
savor the simple things.
Fill yourself with the scent of jasmine flowers;
lose yourself in the flight of birds;
dazzle yourself with the brilliance of the sun;
observe how the clouds change their shapes,
and learn to wait for the rain
without impatience,
for everything comes in its own time.

Halt. Stop yourself and listen.
Guess new sounds,
admire the color of the sky in the afternoon,
and try to count the stars each night . . .
Looking at the vastness,
meet the place you occupy
in the marvelous mystery of creation.
And do not forget to make time
to talk with mother earth.
Discover all that you have in order to teach . . .

HABLA CON LA TIERRA, Y ELLA TE ENSEÑARÁ, JOB 12:8A

Detente. Párate y mira.
Observa, aprecia,
respira, baila, ríe, grita,
goza tu libertad,
disfruta la belleza
de todo lo que te rodea.

Detente. Párate y mira,
saborea las cosas simples,
llénate del aroma de los jazmines,
piérdete en el vuelo de los pájaros,
ciégate con el brillo del sol,
observa cómo las nubes cambian sus formas
y aprende a esperar la lluvia
sin impaciencias,
pues todo llega a su debido tiempo.

Detente. Párate y mira.
Adivina sonidos nuevos,
admira el color del cielo en la tarde,
y trata de contar las estrellas cada noche . . .
Mirando la inmensidad
conocerás el lugar que ocupas
en el maravilloso misterio de la creación.
Y no dejes de hacerte un tiempo
para hablar con la madre-tierra.
Descubrirás todo lo que tiene para enseñarte . . .

—*Gerardo C. C. Oberman*

A moment for writing now might include these writing prompts: Halt, stop yourself and listen . . . Halt, stop yourself and look . . . Halt, stop yourself and smell . . . Halt, stop yourself and taste . . . Halt, stop yourself and touch . . . After each one comes the particularity of one moment, celebrated in God's world.

DOXOLOGY, EARTH DAY

Praise God, above and all around,
Praise God, who is our steady ground,
Praise God, who speaks in ev'ry sound,
The One in whom all love is found.

—*John H. Danner*

Fifty days—longer than Lent, and in many ways, scripturally speaking, also a waiting time. The season of the "big" question: Easter—so what?

Pentecost is the answer.

PENTECOST

Wild Spirit of wind and flame—
you whip up our sometimes humdrum lives
    from out of their complacency!
You fall upon us in unexpected moments:
    turning grief into laughter;
    confusion into motivation.
You surround us in our rush of activities
and settle upon us in our stillness.
    And, in all, you ever entwine
    your holy Breath with our breaths.

You surround us even now, O Spirit.
    offering us peace for our lives,
    pushing us out of our comforts,
    healing us with your hope,

loving us—
    for you are One, O God of delight and justice:
    you are the movement of our lives
    as we seek to embody your Shalom on earth.
    you are the power behind our
    every deed and word,
        even as we pray Jesus' words:
            [Prayer of Our Savior].

—Sharon Benton

• ⬛ •

PRAYER OF CONFESSION

Holy God, the events of Pentecost make us wonder.
Would we have gone to the streets with the others?
Or preferred to stay safe in the upper room?
Would we have followed Spirit-courage out into the light?
Or held back in the security of darkness?
Forgive us when we so often lack the courage to be Your people.
Forgive us for hearing Your Spirit and choosing not to listen.

Assurance of Grace

In all the languages of the world are words of forgiveness. We do not hear
them, till they whisper in the heart. Then we are out the door!

—Jerry Hebenstreit

• ⬛ •

COMMUNION PRAYER, PENTECOST

We give you thanks, God of compassion,
for breathing life into being at the beginning of creation.
We give you thanks for breathing hope into our ancestors' dry bones.
We give you thanks for breathing with us through our brother Jesus.

We give you thanks for breath beyond death, the unbounded mercy
  of resurrection.
We give you thanks for the Wind of the Spirit that breathes in our
  own lungs,
and breathes in us as your One Body.
May we, through this gift of holy breath,
join the Spirit's persistent, insistent, consistent pant for justice.

—*Sonja Ingebritsen*

• •• •

DOXOLOGY, PENTECOST

Praise God, the wind that stirs our hearts,
Praise God, the one who grants fresh starts,
Praise God, the source of each new birth,
Praise God who loves all those on earth.

— *John H. Danner*

• •• •

TRIPTYCH/TRINITY

(to be said in parts or as a whole)

Turn mourning into dancing,
bring hope to my despair,
light up all my darkness,
Father, hear my prayer.

Breathe my eyes from blindness,
heal my bleeding soul,
cleanse my wounded spirit,
Jesus, make me whole.

Give me strength in chaos,
courage in my strife,
wisdom in confusion,
Spirit, come to fill my life.

—*Jerry Hebenstreit*

• ▣ •

Jeff Nelson describes the calling of worship leaders—of pray-ers particularly in the season of Pentecost, the season of many voices, the season of ordinary lives: "As a pastor, I come into contact during any given week with those in the midst of anxious moments from many different causes. When I write prayers (and sermons and Bible studies) these moments inevitably break into my consciousness as I wonder how those dealing with such a diversity of problems will receive what I share, and what they may need to hear. In these times, I think about how they've described their situation to me—what is most difficult for them and where they find reassurance and resources to endure. I strive to be realistic and sympathetic to what they're feeling, and search for hopeful words to share."

AFFIRMATIONS OF FAITH

We believe in a God who is creator and recreator.
We believe in a God who is making all things new:
a God who brings peace to broken hearts, who brings salve to our hurts
    and bruises, who binds up our wounds.
We believe in a God who makes sprouts grow in the scorched and
    wildfire-ravaged places in our lives.
We believe in a God who can take the tough skins, the hard pits,
    the rotting and bruised parts of us and compost them into rich and
    fertile soil where new life can grow.
We believe in a God who walks alongside us through the broken places
    in our lives, a God who is leading us on towards wholeness, a God who
    promises that love will remake the world.

—*Lindsay Ruth Popper*

CELEBRATION SUNDAY

Dancing God,
you whirl through our lives seemingly without taking breath,
spinning around and through our every moment.
You merrily approach then bow to our wall-flower spirits—
your dance partners in creation—
and reach out to take our reluctant hands.

You begin with the slow swaying of our lamentations,
holding us tightly in your arms as we fear to trip and fall
when death and disease advise us to sit this one out;
when overwhelming international news berates us for
"dancing while the world burns."

And still you tease us into the dance of life, O God!
You circle us as in a tango, and,
with a grinning glance over your shoulder,
dare us not to join you.
For even as lives and experiences come to an end,
new life begins—
in infants and newborn relationships,
in resurrected hope and time's healing:
     spring's buds pirouetting in the wind.

And just when we think we can take no more—
     no more joy or sorrow in our filled-up dance cards,
     no more breath for another wondrous round—
then you pull us out again
to dance for the remaking of this world.

—*Sharon Benton*

Often, we wonder what the spiritual practices might be during precious and undervalued Ordinary Time. Vermont pastor Alan Parker turns to music:

"A window into prayer has taken shape in my (almost) daily practice. First, I use music as a way of quieting my mind. I generally prefer music with words that I don't understand. A CD of the Slavyanka Men's Chorus, singing Russian Orthodox liturgical music, plays in the background. One song plays on repeat for an hour or more. I listen, sitting comfortably. Or sometimes I walk the circle around the inside of my home. There is something about the voices that reminds me to talk with God aloud. Not understanding the words keeps me from being distracted by them."

One: We gather as a loving, imperfect, hopeful family of faith,
into God's holy presence.

**Many: We do not forget the cares that weigh us down; we bring them
to God and each other.**

One: We do not forget our joys and pleasures; we know them as
God's gifts, and we share them.

**Many: We do not flee from the troubles of the wider world;
we pray for the strength, patience, and wisdom to bring God's Kin-dom
to this aching world.**

One: We worship together to hear God's still small voice rising above the
noise of our lives.

**Many: We sing praise to God. Our praise is the first step of every sacred
journey. Our praise is the chorus of every step on this holy path.**

—Alan F. Parker

Jerry Hebenstreit says, "I don't really have a well-established prayerful writing practice. I find the period just before sleep (or waking in the middle of the night) is often a time of great inspiration for either starting or redirecting prayers. I also attend a weekly contemplative prayer group, which helps me focus quickly. I also write a lot of songs for a trio I belong to so we can sing them at church. That helps me to get ideas and to hone what I think needs to be said into short, easily understood units."

GATHERING PRAYER

One: O Lord, may our souls rise up to meet you

Many: As the day rises to meet the morning sun.

One: We have traveled to this place on many different paths.

Many: Our journeys are unique and each one is treasured.

One: Yet at this time and place our goal is always the same . . .

Many: To meet You, O God, and learn Your ways. Let us worship God.

—*Jerry Hebenstreit*

• 🐾 •

In a writing moment now, what is the spiritual practice you would choose before writing for a blessing of the animals . . . a communion service to be held outdoors . . . a wedding in a hospital room . . . Sunday afternoon devotionals in the county nursing home? Cody Maynus reflects that the prayer he writes in the campus ministry office where he works is different from the one he writes in the coffee shop. Ultimately, one of the critical questions of this book is whether the spiritual practice that informs our liturgical and personal prayers may be as important as our facility with words or familiarity with text. This is truly a question to consider during ordinary time.

BLESSING OF THE ANIMALS

One: Come and worship God with a "happy tail" that slaps glasses off coffee tables and thumps the linoleum like timpani!

Many: Come and worship God with easy purrs emitted from a puddle of sunlight!

One: Come and worship God with coils slipped around comfortable shoulders!

Many: Come and worship God with pink noses and delicate paws and bright wings and fluid fins!

One: Come and worship the God of all creatures great and small!

Many: Come and worship God as one creation!

—*Sharon Benton*

• ▨ •

A EUCHARISTIC LITURGY FOR A WILDERNESS PEOPLE
The Great Thanksgiving

The Lord is here: God's Spirit is with us.
Lift up your hearts: **We lift them to the Lord.**
Let us give thanks to the Lord our God: **It is right to offer thanks and praise.**

Welcome to the wild place:
the peace of the birds will sing to you,
the leaves of the bush will caress you,
the wind in the trees will move you,

here shadows will play with you,
light will restore you;
welcome to the heart
of love's wilderness.

Although we have sinned and turned away
I went for a run
enjoying the sun
where your pictures come,
barbed wire and beauty
lovers side by side
with explorers
speaking in languages
yet to born.

Eternal God, we remember how, on the night before he died,
your son Jesus took bread,
offered you thanks, broke it, gave it to his friends and said,
Take, eat; this is my body given for you.
Do this to remember me

Then after supper he took the cup,
gave you thanks, and said,

Would you like a drink?
I see you're on a journey;
take a moment,
there is beauty here,
flowers
you might miss
unless you stop—
would you like to share
a cup with me?

This is the blood of the kingdom, shed for you
and for many to forgive sins.
Do this to remember me

Therefore knowing we are surrounded by a great cloud of witnesses we say,
Your mountain looks like a rocket;
the footsteps you see
are from companions
who have climbed with us.

It's hard to see the important thing,
the simple thing,
the central thing,
the place that is pure
that is God in the heart
where the mountain
dances with colour.

O God of heart and mountain and purity,
Send your Holy Spirit
that these gifts of bread and wine
which we receive
may be to us the body and blood of Christ
and that we, filled with the Spirit's grace and power,
may have courage to lead your people
into your holy and life-giving kingdom.

We bless you,
God of the past and of the present,
leading us from death to life,
from despair to hope
today and always. Amen.

Kua akona nei tatou e to tatou Ariki, ka inoi tatou:
E to matou Matua i te rangi
Kia tapu tou Ingoa.
Kia tae mai tou rangatiratanga.
Kia meatia tau e pai ai
Ki runga ki te whenua
Kia rite ano ki to te rangi.
Homai kia matou aianei he taro ma matou mo tenei ra.
Murua o matou hara, me matou hoki e muru nei
I o te hunga e hara ana ki a matou.
Aua hoki matou e te kawea kia whakawaia;
Engari whakaorongia matou e te kino;
No hoki te rangatiratanga, te kaha, me te kororia,
Ake, ake, ake amine.

(Break the bread in silence)

Invitation

Haere mai e te kahui a te Atua.
Tangohia enei kai rangatira a te Karaiti

(After Communion, a time of silence)

Our Lord Jesus Christ be with you to defend you,
within you to keep you,
before you to lead you,
beside you to guard you,
and above you to bless you.

—*Erice C. Fairbrother*

4

A JUICE BAR IN CANA

Contemporary Liturgy

What is weekly worship anyway? In some places, people talk about going to the "meeting house." Many of us attend a church service, either traditional or contemporary. More and more, however, people are seeking a relationship with the Holy Spirit outside of church, and one of the things we must remember when creating our worship, regardless of the locale, is that God's people are everywhere, in every setting, speaking every language, and praying in every conceivable "unprayerlike" way.

If we want to begin to think about worship, especially the slippery lines of a contemporary service, in a more meaningful way, we must first open our eyes to this reality. Christ did not preach from behind a pulpit. He moved. He listened. He spoke and ate with and valued the people he met. He went out and searched to connect God and an impromptu community of faith, and even he probably didn't realize all the places he found it. This is where we must begin—by going out into the world and listening to the people we meet there. Kipp Gilmore-Clough says this about it: "I've been making it a weekly practice to spend a morning at the High Point Cafe. High Point is an institution with deep local roots and a thriving body of regular customers, and it is a decided change of scenery from my dining table or upstairs desk. Every week I look forward to spending my precious hours there, drinking a couple mugs of coffee, eating a cinnamon roll, and working—or not working, depending on who's there to talk with and how interesting the people-watching is.

I had a gradual realization: this is a ritual in the full sense of the word—not only a routine habit, but also a discipline. My regular presence enables me to make new acquaintances, work on friendships, learn of important local undercurrents, experience artwork, become a strand of fabric within a neighborhood tapestry. I accept an invitation . . . to partake of a deep hospitality. That's never a bad practice. I don't know what High Point's owner would make of these words, but I venture them: she is not God, but hers is a place where God may be met."

We are not God, none of us in any of our churches, but we hope that they are places where God may be met. And as Alan Parker writes of his intercessory prayers, "While driving or walking (or sitting in 'a place filled with anonymous strangers'), if I pay heed to what I'm seeing, I find myself asking, 'How is what I see right now a conversation with God?'"

For LL Kroouze DuBreuil, that very question becomes the invitation in her service each week. It is the invitation we offer ourselves, and all who come seeking "a place where God may be met."

INVITATION TO PRAYER

Let us have a conversation with God, first in the words printed in the bulletin, then silently in each heart.

—LL *Kroouze DuBreuil*

Sometimes the place where we meet God matters. Elaine Bolitho is one of several contributors in this book who live in Aotearoa (New Zealand). She shapes this "contemporary" service in her community of worship with a southern hemisphere understanding of season. Patti Rodgers, whose prayer follows, is inspired in the same month of the year to write her prayer from a walk in the woods, a prayer appropriate for community worship for Canadian Thanksgiving, or for any time in the autumn season.

Elaine says: "Our early service each week is a time of meditation. Preparation for me in planning meditations varies, but starts by 'sitting with' God and the lectionary readings for the Sunday for which I am preparing even though the meditation itself is very simple. I also have a collection of books of Celtic (and other) prayers from which I draw inspiration—and sometimes select/adapt passages to commence or end the meditation session.

"The opening is compiled first, and then a blessing to match, and music to introduce each is taken from a collection of CDs chosen for their suitability for meditation.

"In southern hemisphere lectionary material, the month of September is designated for the season of creation—the colour is aqua. As music plays softly, we gather in our prayer room, around a low table with a candle burning in the centre. Copies of the morning's meditation material are ready there for participants to pick up":

MEDITATION FOR THE SEASON OF CREATION

Our God, we are in awe
that You in Your creation live
above us
below us
around us
within us . . .
In the quiet we take time to be aware
of Your loving encircling Godness . . .

There is quiet and there is music.

We say together:
God above us,
God below us,
God around us,
God within us,
You go with us into this day, this week
and every day and week of our lives.
Thank You. We go with You in Your love.
Amen.

—*Elaine Bolitho*

God, remind me to look beneath my feet at the rich world of life going on
down there.

God, remind me to look up, hear the wind whisper and see the arms of the
mother trees outstretched to the sky.

God, remind me that I am not walking to burn calories, but to feed
my soul.

God, remind me that beyond my sight are silent eyes of moose, bear, deer,
and chipmunk watching to see what I will do.

God, remind me to be still and feel resurrection all around me in falling
leaves and growing moss.

God, who are we to build cathedrals?

—*Patti Rodgers*

Grace Paley is quoted in *A God in the House: Poets Talk About Faith*, edited by Ilya Kaminsky and Katherine Towler. "There's a quote, I don't know who said it, 'Find me a God because I am full of prayers.'" People in pews and people online are all full of prayers. We are called to invite the prayers. We are called to introduce the pray-ers to God. We invite some of those prayers not just with words, but by ritual and props. Cheri Holdridge creates liturgy often that reaches out to human senses:

"I sometimes write prayers that intentionally incorporate symbolic objects that have long been used in faith rituals, like oil, water, stones, flame. I am including here three brief prayers I wrote which incorporate different objects":

O God, with this oil, touch _____ gently.

_____ , with this anointing,

(touch her/his eyes gently) may your eyes be blessed for clearer seeing,

(touch her/his ears gently) may your ears be opened for deeper hearing,

(touch her/his lips gently) may your lips be blessed for needful speaking,

(touch her/his forehead, heart, abdomen, hands, feet as it seems appropriate)
may every part of you be filled with God's power and love. Amen.

(Sprinkle person's head with cool water.)
May this water
 refresh you,
 renew you,
 and restore you,
with God's healing grace. Amen.

During a church leadership training session, I passed around a basket of stones, and invited each person to take one. Then I said this prayer:

Feel the texture of your stone;
feel its coolness or warmth in your hand;
feel its firmness and its shape.
These stones remind us
 that, like a rock,
 God is solid under our feet.

And so we pray together,
 Holy God, help us stand firm *(they repeat the line)*
 trusting in your wisdom, *(they repeat the line)*
 growing in goodness, *(they repeat the line)*
 and doing what is right.*(they repeat the line)*
Amen. *(they repeat the Amen).*

—*Cheri R. Holdridge*

Sharyl Peterson also uses tangible objects to touch the elusive spirit. "I have used the following prayer in various settings. I often begin with the quotation from Mother Teresa: 'I am a little pencil in the hand of a writing God, who is sending a love letter to the world.' I also often either give people a brand-new pencil (there's just something spiritual about a brand-new pencil!), or invite them to pick up whatever their preferred writing instrument is, and pray this":

Holy One,
Holy Word.
Write now your message
    of abundant life
in and through me. Amen.

—*Sharyl B. Peterson*

• ◧ •

INVITATION TO PRAYER,
WORDS TO PUT AT EASE EVEN THE NON-PRAY-ERS

We come to prayer together.

This morning some of us feel open to the Spirit,
able to name our joys and sorrows
and place them in God's hands.

Some of us this morning feel
dried up, pinched tight, shut down.

Some of us have the whole Cloud in our brain,
distracted by so much we can hardly sit still.

This is the community of prayer—
those of us with clarity and openness today
have enough "bars" for everyone.
Relax, the rest of you.

Every week some people carry the prayer,
find the deep places,
fill this room with light,
and others are carried, sustained, lit.

—*Maren Tirabassi*

• ◧ •

On World Communion Sunday, we often celebrate with different kinds of bread or short phrases in languages different from our own. Is this reaching the full worship potential of this day? While it's both important and wonderful to celebrate other cultures, it is not enough to pay lip service to our sisters and brothers around the world. Devoree Crist's words that could be a Call to Worship or a Call to Communion explore the heart of this celebration—the extravagant welcome of Christ.

All are welcome at the Lord's table
Jesus bids us come to share in the all-embracing love of God
Those who are at peace with God, those who are struggling in their faith
Those who are hurting, those who feel distant from the Holy
Those who are feeling great joy or contentment
Those who try hard but still stumble, those who are moving in the
   right way today
Those who have trouble forgiving, those who wish to be forgiven
Those who serve the poor, those who are poor
Those who are figuring out how to serve those in need
Jesus calls us as we are to join in the feast with people around the world
All are welcome at the Table of the Lord

—*Devoree Clifton Crist*

• • • •

Lina Andronoviene, who is from Lithuania and teaches in Prague, Czech Republic, reflects on worship, drawing out the commonality of prayer during "attention-seeking" times such as World Communion Sunday or the carols of Advent, as well as all the weeks and months of the year when we communicate faith without any special event:

"I find that praying for people, and writing such prayers, comes out easiest in places and contexts least associated with spiritual practices. This may be a busy bistro at a lunch hour, with lots of noise but a certain deep silence also present in the background. Or on a bustling street with people quickly passing by, where in the speed you still take in the details and the variety in human lives. Or riding a metro and sensing the dramas behind the usual masks of self-control and coolness

. . . Somewhere there, a prayer is born, with or without words; at some point, it is written down; then honed, and perhaps also shown to a person who I hope could relate to it and tell me whether anything seems false or wrong; and—finally there it is. . . ."

Such a practice in the preparation for contemporary worship—taking to the streets before talking to the pews (or the moveable chairs) shakes the jargon out, invites new metaphor in, and always leads the leader to a greater simplicity.

ADVENT

God of people,
God of peace,
God of presence,
As your people
we enter the peace of your presence . . .

There is quiet. There is music.

We say together:
God of peace,
There is no place we can go
where you are not.
You are our God
and we are your people.
You go with us
into this day,
into this week,
into this world—
always.
Amen.

—*Elaine Bolitho*

Ken Sehested responds to a note from a parishioner about the hard first Christmas after the death of her husband. "It doesn't surprise me at all that the holidays are tougher than you thought they would be. This is not at all uncommon when you've suffered such a loss. No doubt you already know this, but you should neither bless nor repress that ache. Just turn to it and say: 'I see you there, Mr. Boogeyman. Stay as long as you like, but you'll get neither a plate nor a bed here:'"

INVITATION FOR SPIRITUAL SHOPPERS

Attention, spiritual shoppers. There are no discounts. No sale prices.
   No 50 percent off summer specials, no bonus miles, no pre-inventory
   clearance or back-to-school savings.
There are no shortcuts to faith, no money-back guarantees, no lifetime
   warranties or last-minute deals.
Every minute is your last. There are no wading pools. The depths are deep
   and turbulence is standard.
Where there is no vision, the people shall perish. Where no wisdom, only
   sorrow and anguish.
But joy awaits every lover's consent to be wed to Beloved's intent.
   Though failure is frequent, pardon is bountiful.
If you want a God-soaked life, move to the margins. Plant sequoias.
   Find an eroded field and stake your soul on its reclamation.
Synchronize your hope to an abandoned child's heartbeat.
   Set your sights on the interest from millennial investments.
Say o'er the clamor of all merchandising madness: Life is not had by what
   is possessed, but only by what has been promised.

—*Kenneth L. Sehested*

INVITATION, ADVENT

Sleigh bells ring . . . are you listening?
Yes, it is all right to listen
to all the cultural sounds of joy

preparing for the Christmas holiday.
Christian people who get too sour-hearted,
too Grinch-stingy,
have a hard time inviting people to the Christ.

But we do here also invite you to listen
to *more* than sleigh bells.
All around you . . .
loneliness murmurs the missing of someone,
financial expectations tap dance a headache,
suppressed mental whimpers identify people with . . .
. . . too much, too much, too much to do.

Pause in the quiet that always precedes holiness—
listen in the spirit to one another
and let us worship God.

—*Maren Tirabassi*

• ◼◼ •

One of the gifts of contemporary worship is flexibility. Because these services often are vastly different from one faith community to the next, there's no reason to feel constrained to a particular order of worship that works for some other "successful growing church" if it doesn't fit the congregation. Play around. Ask for feedback. Some groups may naturally find themselves drawn to a style similar to traditional worship (perhaps with paperless call and response or electronic projection), or they may be traditional in the sense that what happens week to week comes in a predictable pattern. Others may seek constant experimentation. Ultimately, the shape of the service doesn't matter, but the content does. The moments of silence, the connection to the scripture and the mission of the church, the space for both guided reflection and personal contemplation—these are the elements that contribute to meaningful worship.

During Advent, the image of the wreath and candles offers an opportunity to explore a familiar idea with fresh eyes. Think about how it might be possible to stretch the congregation in new directions while remaining grounded in a beloved part of worship.

ADVENT AND CHRISTMAS, "ELEMENTS"

Time of Centering, Advent Season

One: Incarnation of North, ignite in us refining fire.

Many: Enliven us with your regenerative flame.

(*silence*)

One: Incarnation of East, shape us with water.

Many: Increase our surrender to your loving flow.

(*silence*)

One: Incarnation of South, root us in earth.

Many: Reveal to us your embodied presence.

(*silence*)

One: Incarnation of West, breathe in us air.

Many: Animate us by the inspiration of your Spirit.

(*silence*)

First Week of Advent: Fire

Our first Advent candle honors fire.
Fire gives us light.
Fire provides warmth.
Fire clears space for new life.
With our first Advent candle we remember the Star of Bethlehem.
We remember the fire of love in the hearts of those who follow the Star,
    even now.
With Mary, who said yes to the spark of life in her body,
and with the shepherds and magi, who followed the fire sign in the sky,
we light this candle to represent your incarnation through fire.

Prayer of Dedication

Spark of Life and Fire of our bones,
bring us to life through our gifts and our service.
Stoke the most hesitant flame into an inferno of love,

and encourage even our cooling embers
to combust into flames of justice. Amen.

Second Week of Advent: Water

Our first Advent candle honors flame.
Our second Advent candle honors water.
We are all cradled in water,
brought to life in water,
and sustained by water.
We are baptized in water,
refreshed by water,
and receive the gift of Living Water.
With Mary, who carried Jesus in the water of her womb,
and with John, who baptized Jesus in the waters of the Jordan,
we light this candle to represent your incarnation through water.

Prayer of Dedication

Water of Life, Flow of Grace,
break over us and wear away every resistance,
so that our surrender to your generous ways is complete,
and we tumble along in the stream of your will. Amen.

Third Week of Advent: Earth

Our first Advent candle honors flame.
Our second Advent candle honors water.
Our third Advent candle honors earth.
From the dirt on which the donkey trod
to the straw in the stable,
from the baby in the manger,
to the seventh generation beyond our lives,
we see your imprint on the world.
We light this candle to represent your incarnation
through the element of earth.

Prayer of Dedication

You plant your blessings in our lives, Ground of Being,
that we might become blessing to others.
Receive our gratitude for allowing us to participate
in the care of your whole creation. Amen.

Fourth Week of Advent: Air

Our first Advent candle honors flame.
Our second Advent candle honors water.
Our third Advent candle honors earth.
Our fourth Advent candle honors air.
The infant Jesus' first cry will come
from a scoop of breath into his lungs.
Breath of Life, Breath of Being,
may we inhale you deeply and,
like Jesus, cry out
your song of love,
your song of joy,
your song of justice.
We light this candle to represent your incarnation
Through the element of air.

Prayer of Dedication

Animating One, who pours your Spirit into each life,
may the gifts we offer in our gratitude
inspire hope where there is despair and
righteousness where there is injustice.
Send your winds of creativity to disturb
any stagnation of our talent and treasure
so they may become new expressions
of your presence blowing among us. Amen.

Christmas Eve

With creation, we've waited.
With creation, we've prepared.

With creation, we've wondered
where you are sparking new life into creation.

(*Light Advent candle of fire.*)
We've wondered how your current of
persistent love is shaping yet our souls,

(*Light Advent candle of water.*)
We've wondered where in creation and
from what body your body will emerge,

(*Light Advent candle of earth.*)
And we've wondered how your breath will inspire.

(*Light Advent candle of air.*)
We've wondered, all the while held in hope.
Now our hopes are fulfilled.
Our light has come!
(*Light Christmas candle.*)

—*Sonja Ingebritsen*

A wonderful element of being members of a worldwide community of faith is the opportunity to witness the Christmas season through the eyes of people all over the planet. One image we don't often see from the media or church in the United States, however, is what Christmas looks like in the southern hemisphere. Instead of heading into the northern hemisphere's often-dreaded dark days of winter, there it is the blossoming of summer, of long hours of sunshine, and an exuberant atmosphere in which to welcome the Christ Child.

Bright pink lamps are flaming
on the old horse-chestnut tree
and a shining of gold candles
in the kowhai I can see.
The lanterns of the lantern tree

are glowing deeply red
and, here and there, a flame tree
flares bright orange overhead.
Great banks of rhodo blossom
with the colours of the dawn
and buttercups and daisies
gleam like stars across the lawn.
We cannot see the colours
in the darkness of the night
but their beauty is revealed
with the coming of the light.
The light of all our living
is the child of Christmas story,
who shows God's love—its constancy,
its hope and strength and glory.

—*Beverley L. Osborn*

CHRISTMAS, AN OFFERING DEDICATION PRAYER

A town of little consequence became Hope.
Long labor into the night became Peace.
A baby born among cattle became Joy.
A child grown became Love.
If you can use such as these, O God,
use the gifts we bring this night.
Make of them Hope, Peace, Joy, and Love for the world.
And as you transform our gifts of paper and coin,
Gracious One, transform us. Amen.

—*Sonja Ingebritsen*

Following is another Christmas liturgy influenced by summertime in the southern hemisphere.

Over and over
    the Christ is born—
    the seed
of the goodness of God
planted in each new life,
    each singing bird,
    and glowing flower,
    each kindly deed,
    each wide-eyed child.

May we nourish our seeds
into growth and blossoming,
till the whole world shines
    with love.

    For as the earth bursts forth its shoots,
    and as the seeds of a garden sprout and spring up,
    so God will cause goodness and justice
to flourish and flower in full display.
(Isaiah 61:11)

—*Beverley L. Osborn*

Collegiality and meditation are two hidden but necessary ingredients of contemporary worship. When contemporary worship is missing its heart, it is often because these two have been treated as unnecessary.

Collegiality implies prayerful engagement with all of those who are planning worship—clergy and musicians, lay leaders and staff members, band and technical folks. Meditation, on the other hand, suggests time spent in solitary reflection—a difficult but necessary process in the midst of constant chatter and busyness.

A worship service, however "contemporary" the tunes, will feel more like a jumble sale than it will a sacred space if it is only composed of leftovers of worship: five random praise songs, a homily repeated verbatim or cropped shorter from another style of worship, extemporaneous prayers with barely a breath for congregational reflection. Thematic connections can be simple and subtle, but without them, the worship will be not truly share the good news.

Mary Beth Hartenstein reflects on collegiality and meditation a week in advance of worship. "In my current ministry setting, I have a colleague who, if he is doing the reflection for the worship service, assigns me to do the pastoral prayer. In order that we might carry a theme from the opening song to the call to worship to the reflection to the prayer to the close of worship, I meet with him and ask what he has been thinking about regarding the chosen text for that worship service. It is helpful to hear what he has been wrestling with and reflecting about regarding the words, characters, and actions involved in the text."

The service by Cheri Holdridge that follows is an example of how elegant a strong, subtle connection can be when applied to this type of worship. She has constructed her service around a visual, interactive idea that can be accessible regardless of the size of the congregation. Although she has drawn up a solid plan, she has left herself room for interpretation in the moment.

RITUAL: "FORGIVENESS"

Materials needed: electric paper shredder such as used in a home or small office, colored paper, pens or pencils, large clear glass vase

Scripture

Genesis 50:14–21

Key Verse

"Don't you see, you planned evil against me but God used those same plans for my good."

Message Synopsis

Joseph's brothers sold him into slavery, but eventually when the famine came he was in a position to feed his family. God took their act of sin and used it for good. God can take the bad choices of our lives and do amazing things with them. We cannot limit what God can do. One significant part of the story was that the truth had to be told. The brothers had to let go of the secret so that their relationship with Joseph could be restored. When we let go of our sins, and whatever bad choices we have made that we are trying to hide from God, then God can turn our broken lives into something new and good.

Ritual

Invite people to take a small piece of blank colored paper and write down something of which they need to let go: a sin, a bad choice, or something they have done that is hurtful to another person. Have a paper shredder set up at the front of the worship space, near the altar or at the center of your worship area. Let it be there from the beginning of the service and just let people be curious about it. (You will have to deal with the logistics of an electrical cord for the shredder.)

Invite people to come forward and put their paper through the shredder. Explain that as they put the paper in the shredder they are doing it as an act of giving over to God their past act. Explain that throughout the history of the church, this act of letting go has been called confession. We give up our burdens to God because God wants to set us free.

After everyone has had a chance to do this, you might sing a quiet song for a time of transition. You will need to plan for the logistics of the next step. You may want to unplug the shredder and move it out of the way, as you will now want to take the shredded paper out of the shredder and this can be messy. We want to take some of the shredded colored paper and fill the clear glass vase with colored paper (this is why you want a large vase).

After the song, have the leader bring the glass vase filled with the beautiful colored paper and hold it up in front of the congregation with the words: "Do you see, God takes our mistakes and turns them into something beautiful? God takes our broken lives and makes us whole again." Place the vase on the altar or worship table, and then offer a prayer.

Prayer

God of healing and beauty, we thank you, because you look at us and see something beautiful every time. Forgive us when we sin. Forgive us when we hurt one another and when we make mistakes with that have serious consequences. We cannot understand why you want to keep on loving us in all circumstances, but we are so grateful that you do. Thank you, God, for turning all of our mistakes into opportunities for blessing. Amen.

—*Cheri R. Holdridge*

• ▦ •

Lent is a season when we face seriously the Sabbath. It is a time when we must reach even deeper into ourselves to find a place of restful contemplation, and we must be prepared to lay that part of ourselves out for others as well. This is a time to choose between those activities that are truly meaningful, both inside the church and out, and those that remove us further from God. Matthew Braddock says:

"Our church schedules a monthly "Sabbath Sunday," when there are no meetings, votes, or agendas—a day my overprogrammed, overachieving congregation can walk out the church doors and find renewal in creation. It's a struggle. Some churchgoers like it. Some want more meetings. Most are ambivalent. I, too, struggle to find time for rest, simplicity, freedom, and gratitude. Glimpses of Sabbath are found in heartfelt yearnings for rest in the midst of demanding work and prayers to enjoy the simpler life."

The idea of taking Lent beyond its calendar boundaries is a beautiful one. It is at the core of what we are trying to do with our prayers and worship here. It is an opportunity for us to bring the Sabbath to all days, and to nurture it within all people.

ASH WEDNESDAY

Ash-bearer God,
who gives me insomnia to remind me how old I am
with all my sins of untaken chances,
walk among the frail of all ages
with forgiveness
and the hope of holy days,
turning our cinders to embers. Amen.

—*Maren Tirabassi*

IN DIFFICULTY

When the moon fails to reflect sun's light
and we are left in the depths without stars' guidance—
come to us as sound calling us forward.
When our grasping hands
find no purchase in a freefall—
come to us as the letting go.
When all we need is a listening ear
to hear our hearts' tellings—
come to us as the silence
more still than we can disturb.
(*silent prayer*)

—*Sharon Benton*

INVITATION, LENT

Lent loves you.
Lent loves you without your clothes.
Lent loves you without your education or job.
Lent loves you without your family and friends,
 without your homes,
 without your Crate and Barrel, IKEA, Dollar Store, thrift shop stuff.
Lent loves you without your tattoos,
 without the ring you aren't wearing anymore,
 without Facebook or LinkedIn.
Lent loves you,
 if you are young, without SAT scores,
 if you are old, without your memory.

Lent loves you . . . without . . . can you name something?
(*People share ideas*)

Lent is the name of the season when we celebrate—yes, celebrate!
   God loving us, bare and simple.

Some of us remind ourselves of this love
by consciously letting go one or more things for six weeks.

Some of us try to quiet all the inside and outside critics
so we can be open to God.

Some of us feel full, abundant—
and want to give some time or energy or money away.

Fasting, prayer, and alms are the old-fashioned tags
for things we do in Lent.

Join us . . . Lent loves you without your clothes.
God loves you always!

—*Maren Tirabassi*

• •• •

Lindsay Popper says, "As a poet, my writing practice centers around having a note-book with me wherever I go so that I can jot down lines, ideas, images, and questions as they come to me. I gather such bits over a period of time, and then craft them into poems later when I'm at my computer. I used the same approach with these prayers, which I worked on during Lent while I was disconnected from Face-book and praying the Daily Offices from the Episcopal Book of Common Prayer. I was steeped in the language and tradition of collects, and I carried that sense with me as I walked through the world, staying sensitive to the situations or people I felt led to pray for."

Entering into Holy Week, from the ebullience of palms waving to the somber reflection on the depth of Christ's sacrifice, it's possible to find ourselves hung up on our own jagged, human edges. What have we learned during Lent? What have we sacrificed, not just for ourselves, but for our brothers and sisters in the global community? Have we offered up prayers on their behalf, or only our own? Have we considered that our struggles, and the struggles of strangers, are equal in the eyes of God? Have we mourned for those we've lost during our journey? This week, in suspension between Lent's holiness and the celebration of Easter, we consider both the joy and pain.

OPENING PRAYER—THE SPICE OF LIFE

God of the seasons—cayenne spring,
basil summer, nutmeg autumn,
winter of savory and thyme—
who gave us this sweet full moon day of thaw,
remind us that Lent is
the lengthening light of the sun,
the path from sharing a kid's lunch
to breaking bread and bitter herbs . . .
the way we still taste and see
that you are good. Amen.

—*Maren Tirabassi*

• •• •

PRAYER FOR GOOD FRIDAY

Christ, tongue bright with vinegar,
who has done nothing wrong—
not war or cancer,
not tsunamis, Alzheimer's,
traffic accidents killing children—
remember us,
as you hang suspended from our pain,
remember me,
before I forget myself. Amen.

—*Maren Tirabassi*

• •• •

Here are placed, in a Holy Saturday "position" in the liturgical year, two memorial pieces. Both may be used with many different names, and as a reflection on that suspension of holiness, the quiet place before Easter.

Go with our love, dear _____ . Your stories will still be told; your love is built into us; you will always be in our hearts.

—*Beverley L. Osborn*

• ◖◗ •

Lord, you posted Taurai Muteyo to our address on earth.
Today after twenty-seven years you have sent your loyal postman
to post that same letter to another permanent address.
Thank you, Lord,
for giving us this beautiful letter to read.

—*Lancelot Muteyo*
*(in loving memory of his brother Taurai Muteyo, 22 April 1985–26 August 2012,
who passed away in a traffic accident in Harare, Zimbabwe)*

• ◖◗ •

Easter worship is as simple as sunrise observance or as elegant as trumpet fanfare and banks of lilies. Contemporary worship, on this holy day, will have a flavor of each.

God, you call to us from the throats of many
The many who have come this Easter morning

Our faith rustles with its very newness
As it does each year, despite the agony of Christ,
Despite the suffering born in our mortal frailty

Because like Christ, with his vulnerable humanity,
We have a spirit, each of us, great enough to rise

Great enough to roll away the stone
And find our faith renewed

—Maria Mankin

• •• •

MORNING KARAKIA (MAORI WORD FOR "PRAYER")

The West Coast of the South Island of New Zealand is a geographically dramatic sort of place with fantastic scenery. As one drives along its length, one passes through many areas where the strip of land between mountain and sea is very narrow. With mountains and cliffs in such close proximity, it's not surprising that fossicking for stones in riverbeds and on the beaches is endlessly fascinating. The variety of colours and combinations and rock types is amazing and it's awe inspiring also to think what life changes have happened to the coloured stones we can pick up and admire.

Once they were part of huge mountains. Those mountains have been subjected to volcanic and earthquake changes, to the grinding of tectonic plates, to the relentless winds and snows and rains and searing sunshine of thousands of years. They'll have experienced ice ages, been buried in glaciers, been gouged and broken by swift flowing rivers and voluminous waterfalls, and they'll have been subjected to the enormous pressures that meld different kinds of stone together. Great chunks will have broken off and gone bouncing down cliffs and, gradually, smaller and smaller stones will have become separate entities, tumbled in rivers, washed by sea, hurled about in water, scoured by sand and wind.

When we hold a stone in our hands, we hold the most enormous history and seldom realize how precious an article we see and feel. I think it's a bit the same with humans. In the beginning, we are taught there was God— the creative spirit, the essence of love—whatever name sits comfortably for you. In the beginning was God and all creation comes from that one life source. Everything that is must, therefore, be part of that energy, that essence, changed and shaped by many circumstances over millions of years. When we look at a human being and reach out to touch, there, too, we should sense the most enormous history and the preciousness of each individual.

Choose a stone now, hold it in your hand, look at it, feel it, respect it, be awed by it—and then think of yourself—all that has gone into the making of you as the capable, special person you are. When you are done wondering and being awed and grateful, look round at your companions in this room and be thankful for all that has gone into making them the gifted, knowledgeable, caring people they are, people who have honed and polished skills.

Take your stones home and hold them sometimes if you're feeling a bit low. Remember how special they are, what they've endured to become what they are, and how special you and all human beings are—and be thankful.

—*Beverley L. Osborn*

• ▪▪ •

CALL TO WORSHIP, PENTECOST

(*with worship team all participating and then the gathered congregation*)

One: Holy Spirit, come.

Add voice two: Send your flame as you did before.

Add voice three: To set our hearts on fire for you,

Add voice four: That we might be filled with that divine love you so share so abundantly.

Many: Let us be Your church to live our faith and share your love with all creation.

—*Devoree Clifton Crist*

• ▪▪ •

Without the structure of the sacred as dictated by the liturgical calendar, it can be easy to fall into a prayerful worship rut. Maybe it's time for the stewardship campaign, or the children are completing Sunday school program year—there are any number of things that take place during and after Pentecost that lead us away from collegiality and meditation. It can seem less important during these "ordinary days," when, truly, this is when we must search hardest for the holiness in our lives.

This is when we must be active in exploring the boundaries of our faith in worship. When Beverley Osborn reflects on her own spiritual practice in preparation for prayer, she says, "For me, prayer is a bit like a rain dance—a gathering up and intensifying of energy to achieve a positive result—but in prayer, that energy is joined to the will and love of God." The question then must be: How can we join to the will and love of God during ordinary time?

PRAYERS OF PRAISE FOR MODERN TIMES

In urban canyons, rural Main Streets,
suburban courts, and country lanes,
you are there, O God. We praise your name!

We plumb the ocean depths, we sail the skies, we touch outer space
and always we see your hand, O God.
You are our Creator and Sustainer.

As we see farther and farther into the universe,
your glory grows with each new discovery.
Boundless is your majesty, O God.

—*Jerry Hebenstreit*

• ▨ •

Daniel Ross-Jones wrote, "Working with teenagers and young adults in Silicon Valley, I am constantly bombarded with 'the next big thing.' I always try to pay attention to the tools being presented to me as possible connecting points, because these are currently serving as a sort of town square where people build community and seek out one another."

Listen to one another. We can shape a commission.

We are constantly bombarded by the "next big thing." Let us pay attention to the tools that are given to us—as new as the next app, as old as the trowel to help a neighbor plant bulbs. These are our possible connecting points. These are the ways we build community and seek out one another. Connect, build, seek.

We are constantly bombarded by the "next big thing." Let us use it but not lose ourselves in the rush from now to tomorrow. Connect, build, seek, and remain whole.

INVITATION TO PRAYER

Close your eyes; reach out your hand.
Imagine a white cane in your hand.
It is as smooth as a psalm,
with a grip as never-let-go
as childhood bedtime words.
The tip is Amen—
Amen to everything you are,
and everything your life touches.

This is the white cane of prayer.

Tap forward
feel the edges of what you need to pray.

When you stand before crossings and crosses,
know that you are safe.

Feel your way, listen your way,
walk your way into God.

—*Maren Tirabassi*

CLOSE OF DAY

We are about to go back to our homes now, to the places where we work, relate to the people around us, live our daily lives. Enjoy all the people whom you meet and be aware that, as you tumble round ideas, words, actions and feelings, like stones, wonderful things may come to light, pressures may meld something new and beautiful, and sparks of genius may fly!

—*Jerry Hebenstreit*

5

A FLASH MOB OF ANGELS

*Invitation to Spiritual
Practices for Individuals
and Small Groups*

Devoree Crist, a layperson who works as a writer and retreat facilitator for youth and adults in the St. Louis, Missouri, area wrote, "Prayer is very personal and as such should reflect the person praying when one is writing prayers for other individuals or for a larger group. Taking into consideration the nature of the person or the group's needs, one still speaks in one's own voice, from the heart."

There are many excuses people have to avoid writing prayers (from "that's the clergy's job" to "writing's not from the heart"). This attitude is a barrier to liturgy becoming truly "the work of the people" for those who are already in the pews and the ones who may only stop by once. This is partially because written prayers can come off as insincere, and partially because they require tackling emotional issues that may be sensitive or disturbing. It can be easier to say nothing, to put the whole thing aside for a more experienced person rather than risk praying "the wrong thing."

Even clergy, however, can and do underestimate the power of prayer in the context of worship. It is often during the briefest elements of the service, these bridges of explanation and welcome, when newcomers are most touched, but many pastors and worship leaders consider music, sermon, and pastoral prayer as central. No matter who we are, lay or clergy, we should not underestimate the blessing that is fresh, the confession that is poignant, the invitation that speaks words as new and unexpected as a flash mob. Faith can struggle and revive itself in the most unusual places, in company we never expect. It doesn't take an ordination to pray—it only requires mental space to hear God's call.

The people who responded to the invitation to become a part of this book knew that prayer writing was a part of it; however, even they were surprised by their experiences. Molly Baskette says:

"Writing these prayers felt a lot more personal than I thought it would. I picked topics that seem to come up a lot among the people in my church but are topics that they are reluctant to bring to me because they feel shy or ashamed, or don't think they're 'important' enough to merit pastoral attention or prayers.

"When I wrote the actual prayers, though, I couldn't just think of the people I knew who had suffered in these ways—I had to go back in time to when I had suffered, and be the age I was then, and 'know' only what I knew of God and life then—not how things would eventually turn out. Which is what prayer is for, anyhow. Prayer is not a logical, common-sense advice-giving session. It's the cry of someone who can't see a way out of a situation, who is reaching a hand out of the depths and hopes there is someone to grasp and pull from the other side."

A written prayer is neither more nor less "true" than an extemporaneous prayer, a memorized prayer from a treasured tradition, a sung or danced prayer, breath prayer, prayer in tongues, the open space of meditation, the embodied prayer of, say, a runner, a gardener, a craftsperson, a dishwasher, or a witness for justice. The written prayer is one form of prayer that can be easily shared in a worship context and through social media, which are two of the settings that particularly interest us in this book.

Unfortunately, it can be easy to "phone it in" when writing prayers. A clergy person hits computer keys to fill in a bulletin space while thinking about the upcoming hospital visit, committee agenda, sermon, or wedding couple. A friend e-mails someone who has recently received a difficult diagnosis or damaged a personal relationship and falls into the trite familiarity of Internet prayer-chain language. A person decides to submit a prayer for publication and finds a pesky ego in residence. Because this book was intended to be a conversation about prayer rather than just a resource volume, we asked that the writers also engage in a spiritual practice for writing prayers of intercession and liturgy (their own practice or a new one that we suggested) and then reflect on the experience.

Some of the practices that follow were sent out to the writers and some are new. The first eight practices are directed at personal prayer writing, with some adaptation for groups, and the later ones are suggestions for working with small groups, such as study circles, youth groups, deacons, or at retreats. Devoree Crist has often focused on this set of practices: "I prepare myself to work with groups by centering myself on God and asking for guidance. I like to acknowledge who is in the group and make adjustments based on the makeup of the group. Though it is hard to begin, after a while prayers flow. Some of the youth suggest they don't know what to say but after telling them to just talk to God, it becomes doable. The language isn't always flowery but it is meaningful and genuine."

The practices we have decided to share are only a small percentage of the possibilities available. We wanted to avoid ideas familiar from other sources (for example, centering prayer, labyrinth practice, or lectio divina). We have chosen to invite prayer by combining simple elements—nature and scripture, friends and strangers, time and space. These are simply jumping off points, openings, and invitations to begin.

Prayer Writing Practices for Individuals
Not in a mirror, but face to face

Go to a place filled with strangers who are at least temporarily stationary—a coffee shop, a food court in a mall, a bus terminal, an emergency room waiting area, a Little League game. You don't know the stories within these lives, though you may be able to guess in some cases. One by one, pray for each person there. Now choose one person and take a mental picture so that you can remember and pray for this person after you return to where you will write the prayer down. Pray in as much detail as you can . . . "God, touch the life of the man in the green sweater with his hair thinning and the little tattoo on his left wrist. May he have . . . unexpected good news, reconciliation with the person he is most uncomfortable with, a sense of pride in the work he does today. Let him remember to say 'I love you' to someone dear and . . ." You get the idea! Experience your empathy growing.

Of all the prayer suggestions sent out for this book, this was the one that spoke to most people. Lindsay Popper wrote, "The skeletons of these prayers were scribbled down in city parks, prison waiting rooms, dark concert halls, outside of churches, and in friends' living rooms, and then they were edited and condensed into collect-like prayers reflecting the topics that resonated most strongly with me."

The coffee shop is the most obvious of these locations to choose—it is a place of individuals looking at their laptops and pairs in the midst of conversations with just a word or two audible over the hum of the rest of the room; it is also a place where scribbling reflections is acceptable.

Expand this spiritual practice by choosing a different place each week. Do this for a liturgical season, perhaps Lent or Eastertide. Some suggested locations are listed above in the original assignment; here are a few more:

- Go to a public library in the afternoon. Pray the room. Identify at least one person who is homeless getting out of the weather. Identify one latchkey kid.

- Go to an unemployment office. Pray for the clients. Now pray for the employees, who can't do everything, who have grown some hard heart-edges, who wilt or bristle when they are the targets of pent-up frustrations.

- Now try the Department of Motor Vehicles. Look past the lines and recognize that those are human faces sitting behind the counters.

- Go to the local Humane Society or SPCA. Walk around the cages for adoption and read the tags. Pray for the animals, looking at their faces. Now pray for the people behind the animals. These animals are here because of death and divorce, losing a house, not having the money to pay for a pet, and living a lifestyle so busy there isn't time for fur. Some of these animals got lost and families are crying for them.

The trees of the fields will clap their hands

Find a familiar or new place of natural power or beauty; settle in to reflect on this place and how God is speaking to you. Bring your list of prayer concerns with you. Although there are many prayers we pray for creation—in thanks for its beauty and bounty, in hopes of its preservation, in lament for its destruction—this is not that list. You are bringing your paper-congregation outdoors. Simply and prayerfully read the whole list. Let people sit on the rocks or the sand, imagine them leaving their kitchens, cubicles, dorm rooms, and dog walks to join you in this place. Stay long enough that you know which prayer you want to write. Start writing it here by hand on the back of the paper (of course you can smooth it out on your computer later).

Writing on the heart

Reflect on these passages of scripture about writing until one of them moves you. Spend a couple of days letting that passage surprise you. Take a line from it and stick it on a screensaver, put a post-it note on the bathroom mirror, or bake a cake and write it in frosting! Yoga? Breathe it in your down dog. Treadmill? Imagine it as a "holy ear bud." Pray for this scripture to inform your writing, choose an idea, topic, or person from your list of prayer concerns, and then write a longer prayer from what has come from this time of meditation.

SCRIPTURES

- Jeremiah 31:31–34—writing on the heart
- Deuteronomy 6:4–8—writing holy words on just about anything
- Ezekiel 2:8–3:3—eat your words
- Ecclesiastes 12:12—there's enough of a good thing
- Daniel 5:1–5—a handwriting on the wall
- Habakkuk 2:2—write it so plain a runner can read it
- John 1:1—a Word before we had any walls

- John 8:1–11—especially verses 6–8, the holiness of dust-writing
- John 20:30–31—why we write any of it
- John 21:24–25—there are so many more stories!
- Revelation 10:8–10—the bitter and the sweet
- Revelation 21:5—write only what is trustworthy and true

And there was evening and there was morning and God saw that it was good

This is a practice that allows your prayer to "steep." Explore the gift of time. Choose a topic from your prayer list and pray mentally on it for six days. You may know someone in the chosen situation, you may have had the experience yourself, or you may be stretching your imagination. Intentionally pray differently each day and explore moving from bland platitudes to more specific hopefulness. An imagined person may become more real for you. Do not be surprised if you meet such a person during the course of the week. Rest from these prayers on the seventh day. On the first day of the new week write your prayer.

Vince Amblin used this spiritual practice to pray for someone he knew in a different way every day. "I believe it was this multifaceted exploration (as well as the challenge to be brief) that led me to a more imagistic and metaphorical prayer. It seemed impossible to capture the breadth of my prayer for her in straightforward prose without going on for pages."

Writing the Psalms

The Psalms are the ultimate template for prayer. They are the prayers of the Jewish people and they have been the prayer book and the hymnbook of the church. They are, however, so familiar that their sharp edges and high pinnacles have become dulled from overfamiliarity. Here are two ways to invite them to be a fresh spiritual practice:

1. *Responding to the Psalms in haiku*—a six-month to one-year practice. The haiku is a form of Japanese poetry, or actually a part of a form, that is familiar enough and brief enough to become a reflection tool. Haiku is defined as a three-line poem with the first line having five syllables, the second seven, and the third five again, although Japanese poets insist that the form

can be flexible in its count—it is a guide and not a recipe. A haiku is also defined by having some kind of twist or surprise in it.

Read a psalm each day and respond by writing a haiku. This may be a retelling of it, a personalization of it, or a reaction to it. Of course, many psalms are long and haiku are very short. The struggle to respond to this difference is valuable. Every once in a while, two haiku will be called forth, maybe at different times in the day—keep them both. Every once in a while, the psalm may naturally fall into two sections—take one per day. Psalm 119 will probably need a whole week!

Perhaps it seems important to skip one of the psalms and go to the next one. Sit and reflect on the reason for doing this. You may be avoiding what the psalm calls forth. Stay with the psalm. It may be that it simply is not speaking to a personal situation. Go on to the next one then. If that one seems a perfect fit, reflect on it, and continue to the next the following day. If it does not fit, return to the abandoned psalm and write a haiku. You may well discover the reason later.

2. *Writing from the Psalms*—a one-week to five-week kaleidoscope practice. This spiritual practice needs a friend—a writing friend or a soul friend. The actual process involves reading and reflecting on a single line from a psalm every day. These psalms may have beautiful language but should not be the top five favorites that are so well known the pen will automatically gravitate to the original language. Five suggested psalms with their specific lines are listed below to get the idea going.

Your friend will copy the chosen psalms out and cut them into single lines. He or she will give you those lines—one psalm a week—in a grab bag. Daily, you will pull out a line, reflect on it, and write a prayer, a call to worship, an invitation to communion, a benediction—some small piece of liturgy that embeds that line, or your contemporary restating of it. The following day another line is used (and so on, for five days). At the end of the five days, your friend will tell you what the psalm was, and you can read the original psalm and the prayer or liturgy that has emerged from the practice.

As a small group exercise, you may also take an entire psalm, cut it into one-line segments (cutting out pieces you know won't scan with your group), then offer it to a youth group, board of deacons, study circle, or evening gathering of friends in a grab bag. They each have a short period of time to write a prayer that embeds the line or the idea in the line before all share their prayers. Finally, read to the group the original psalm and allow them to discover the depth of contemporary meaning their embellishments have brought to this ancient template of prayer.

List of psalms lines for the individual practice:

- Psalm 61: 2a, 2b, 3, 4a, 4b, 5a
- Psalm 63: 1, 5, 6, 7, 8
- Psalm 104: 2b–3, 12, 13, 16, 25, 33
- Psalm 116: 6, 8, 9, 11, 13
- Psalm 146: 2, 5, 7, 8, 9

List of psalms for the group practice:

- Psalm 8,
- Psalm 32
- Psalm 91
- Psalm 148

If the group does not know the psalms very well, Psalms 1, 42, 84, 121, 139 work well.

Sabbath writing

Sabbath writing is writing by hand, rather than on the computer, once a week and reflecting on that practice. It seems simple, but in fact there are many ways in which this deepens prayer writing. There is a different tactile sense in using a pen or a pencil. For many people now, the most common writing by hand is on an electronic pad for a credit card transaction. Sabbath writing is writing that does not buy anyone anything. It is also writing that might need to be typed into a computer the following day to be shared, thus calling for the experience of doing something twice—much hated in contemporary experience! That second writing is also an opportunity to deepen the experience.

Finally, Sabbath writing invites tactile playfulness. Write on different kinds of paper. Write with pencil, mechanical pencil, fountain, pen, ballpoint pen, marking pen. Write with ink and brush. Study just a little bit of calligraphy. Experience the beauty of Arabic writing, of Asian scripts.

What cultures use pictograms? The early Egyptians, the Chumash people of California, the Pacific Northwest First Nations people of Alaska and Canada. What about the International Standard public information symbols. Write by pictograph. This is different than drawing, sketching, or watercolor. Writing by pictograph involves creating some kind of personal alphabet—as simple as first initials for people or a sun or a fish or a cross for God, though potentially, you may choose to create something much more complex.

Sabbath writing also might involve sketching or watercolor!

Play with Sabbath writing, but in deeply serious ways. Here is one simple example: write a confession in pencil. Take an old-fashioned square eraser and erase it. The words are gone but the paper itself is distressed, slightly damaged. The eraser is stained. Resharpen the pencil so it has the fresh "assurance of grace" point to write on, but notice that the pencil is shorter.

Perhaps a physical journal or notebook for handwriting is a comfortable way to keep track of this. Perhaps a recipe box could hold index card–sized pieces of paper. Perhaps a roll of paper . . .

Of course, Sabbath writing can also be writing about Sabbath, based on one of the four biblical strands—the creation, the liberation law-giving of Exodus, the prophetic reintroduction of Sabbath integrity, or Jesus' claim that Sabbath is meant for human well-being.

An underlying important piece of this spiritual practice is that we must practice Sabbath before practicing Sabbath writing.

Prayer as jigsaw

Sometimes it seems like prayer comes in pieces. With jagged or smooth holes, it needs to be fit in, but we turn and turn it around, and still it is a puzzle. This practice plays with that imagery for ordinary life moments, like waiting in traffic or standing in a checkout line.

Find puzzle pieces to keep in one of two small bowls by your door (second-hand puzzles are easily available in thrift stores or online). Stick a couple in your pocket when you leave the house. When you have those unattached moments, take the piece in your hand and feel it. Feel the edges, the smooth and rough surface. Think of it as a prayer, though you don't know for whom or for what. A name will come into your mind—it may be someone you know, a name that feels random, or someone you heard mentioned at church. Write the name on the back of the puzzle piece. You still do not know how your prayer fits into that person's life, but you know it does. You are just holding it. Touch it every once in a while during the day. Perhaps some words will come. When you get home, put the puzzle piece with the name in the second bowl. Occasionally, sort through these names and lift them up to God.

Need prayer? Write your own name on the back of a jigsaw puzzle piece and put it somewhere that speaks to you—a communion table, a rack of votive candles, the center of a labyrinth, a bench at a scenic overlook, or on a shelf in a bookstore. It will be found.

Runners, swimmers, walkers of dogs

The methodical, repetitive movement of physical exercise soothes the mind and allows prayer to lift into consciousness. Meditation practice often uses the categories "sitting meditation" and "walking meditation." Let go of the specifics of those practices. Choose a physical activity you already love. Turn off any distractions—perhaps the audio book or the playlist, the worry agenda or the advance planning. That alone is a prayerful action and lovingly intentional.

There are two directions to invite your body-led mind. One is for personal prayer. Present, as simply as possible, a question or a problem, then be open to the Spirit. This is, in some sense, the opposite of brainstorming. It may be a frequent practice as feet walk a labyrinth or fingers follow a rosary, but what about those hours we spend on the treadmill, the Stairmaster, the theraband routine?

The second direction is to be open to what is usually called "inspiration." Interestingly enough, inspiration means "breathing in," and that is best remembered during exercise. You may see people during your run. Pray for them. You may be filled with memories. Pray through them. Liturgy, ultimately a shared rhythmic activity, emerges out of repetitive movement more than it does sitting behind a desk. Whisper it out loud. Remember, if you can, and write it when you return home.

Whatever closes your exercise session—hot tub, warm shower, deep drink of water, or quick sip of an energy beverage—is a time for intentional gratitude.

Prayer writing practices for small groups

Devoree Crist shares her experiences working with small groups in prayer: "We spend time sharing concerns with one another and then the youth work individually on a prayer they would like to share. Sometimes they work together in a subgroup to contribute to the whole. After prayers are written, people read them aloud in the group during worship or pray as a group. We have considered posting prayers on Facebook. I find it fulfilling to share such a spiritual activity with young people. They always amaze me with their words and the depth of their thinking about their faith."

Sometimes facilitators of small groups that are not actually defined as "writing" groups hesitate to share a writing activity, particularly writing prayer. A wonderful aspect of these activities, however, is that they involve a pause for everyone to have a response, not just the most extroverted participants. While only a few may choose to share aloud what they have written, each member of the group has his or her own writing to reflect upon later.

A challenge may be that people who don't consider themselves "writers" are self-conscious about their abilities, either because they have not traditionally considered writing to be one of their gifts or because it has been a long time since they last "wrote." Of course, when we really consider this excuse, we realize it probably has not been a long time since we've texted, tweeted, posted, or e-mailed—all of which are forms of writing! Identifying prayer writing with these more fluid, spur-of-the-moment forms rather than blue books, college essays, obituaries, or reference letters is a simple way to remind all people, "writers" or not, about how familiar and comfortable the written language can be.

Using nonpermanent surfaces may also help to break down some anxiety people have with trying something new. Electronic tools like tablets or laptops are one way to do this, but there are others that may provide a gentler shift of spiritual energy. Give everyone a paper plate and ask them to write grace for people with whom they regularly share a meal. This is simple and nonthreatening, but also very personal. Push just a little harder and invite them to include in the prayer at least one person whom they miss, who has been at the table and is not now because of death or distance. Then, with this prayer in their hearts and hands, ask them to turn their plates over and each write a prayer for Holy Communion. This is not an exercise in trying to remember what the prayers in a particular denominational liturgy say, but an opportunity to write grace for a larger family table.

Another possibility is to cover a table with white or brown paper so that everyone is writing on the same surface. This larger format works well for those whose natural creative expression is artistic rather than verbal. A prayer can be a sketch or a cartoon strip or even words written and then overwritten with a neighbor's. Sand on a beach, sidewalk chalk, banana skins, a strip of fabric to be braided into a rug, the palm of one's own or another's hands—all of these may become writing surfaces for prayer.

One last preliminary concern when using prayer writing as a group activity is clear instruction about the public disclosure of the prayers. People want to know before they begin whether everyone will read aloud, or only those who choose to do so. Will people turn to one neighbor and share what they have written, or will the prayers go into an anonymous pile to be read without identification? Maybe the prayers will be laid face down in an offering basket and prayed over without detail as a group. Any of these ideas are acceptable, but, if it isn't clear at the start of the exercise, participants will waste spiritual energy wondering about "delivery" when they should simply be reflecting.

Here are some "beginnings, some promptings for prayer":

Band-Aid on the globe

Everyone receives a Band-Aid and holds it for five minutes while looking at a globe in the center of the circle. After the meditation (or during it) they write a word or a tiny prayer on the Band-Aid. It might be a country, a place of conflict, or a country of origin. It could also be a global issue, such as hunger or AIDS. To close, each person has the opportunity to put the Band-Aid on the globe and share the prayer aloud. Clearly explain that duplicate prayers, such as "world hunger," or "refugees," are acceptable.

Familiar template prayer

There are prayer and blessing forms that are so woven into culture that they invite both the church-familiar and the mildly curious to engage in prayer. There is simplicity in the initial fill-in-the-blank writing but a potential for ongoing deep reflection.

THE SERENITY PRAYER (a shortened version familiar from many recovery groups and often ascribed to Reinhold Niebuhr):

God grant me the serenity to accept the things I cannot change, the courage to change the things I can, and the wisdom to know the difference. Amen.

God, grant me the serenity to _____.
God, grant me to courage to _____.
God, grant me the wisdom to _____. Amen.

By using the full sentence three times, the one praying is allowed to reflect on three different things in his or her life rather than aspects of one.

GAELIC TRADITIONAL BLESSING

May the road rise up to meet you.
May the wind be always at your back.
May the sun shine warm upon your face,
the rains fall soft upon your fields, and, until we meet again,
may God hold you in the palm of God's hand.
May your road _____.
May the wind _____.
May the sun _____.
and the rains _____.
Until we meet again _____.
and may God _____.

Other culturally significant prayers that may be approached with gratitude might include the Navajo prayer for the conclusion of the Blessing Way or the prayer of St. Francis.

A biblical possibility includes exploring vocationally diverse metaphors for God, using the twenty-third psalm, which begins "The Lord is my shepherd." The full psalm as a model is too complex, but it suggestively presents in the minds of people. Try "God is my parole officer" . . . "God is my high school teacher" or "my preschool teacher" . . . "God is my physical therapist" . . . "God is my flight attendant" . . . "God is my public defender" . . . "God is my EMT."

A similar idea is to engage the Beatitudes, looking at Jesus' unexpected choices—the poor in spirit, the meek, the persecuted—and the reversal of expectations in the blessing:

Blessed are people in hospice, for they are closer to God.
Blessed are people in prison, because they have a chance to begin again.
Blessed are people in recovery, for they are seeking a silver lining.

Christmas prayer chain

Here's a simple idea for teens and young adults. Give each participant three red and three green strips of paper. They will write prayers on each of the strips. Each may write a name, a sentence, or paragraph about an issue or a category. Go around the circle six times. A person may staple a strip prayer side out and read it aloud, or just staple it with the prayer on the inside. Let the group know it is important to hear some spoken and to receive some in silence. It is not "better" to read them aloud, because many people for whom we pray do not want their concerns publicized, but they may still want to be part of the chain. Hang the chain on a tree.

Holding a piece of the crèche

Mix several crèches with diverse racial ethnic features in a bag and have each person draw one out to feel and reflect upon for five minutes without writing; then allow them five minutes to free-write. The participants may pray for a contemporary person in a similar situation—an unwed mother, motel owner,

TSA employee, foster parent, or anyone awaiting or receiving life-changing news. This may encourage a dialogue between the writer, God, and the person who is being prayed for, or it may be as simple as a few words of prayer for the person this brings to mind (or for the writer). "Sometimes I feel like the magi. In the middle of the night everything on my journey is so clear, just like starlight, but when morning comes I just can't find my way."

Consider the lilies and the onions . . . and the corkscrews

Some people are stimulated to pray by word-oriented prompts, but many are more tactile. To touch or smell an object may transport them to a place of prayer in a way they hadn't anticipated. There are several ways to engage this aspect of the prayer life. The first is to consider a natural object. Place in a basket an onion and a leaf, a stick, a shell, a stone, an apple, a potato, a feather, dog fur, a flower, a bulb. Pass the basket and have each person choose an object and write a prayer after holding and considering that object for several minutes. Instructions may include inviting not only the sensory exploration but also memory exploration.

Another way to share these is to include both natural and human-made objects (those listed above, plus a mitten, a spoon, a pair of glasses, a candle). Mix these objects and put them in paper lunch bags so that the recipients do not know what they will receive; it is often easier to simply respond to what has been given than to be frustrated after choosing a metaphor that will not come.

A helpful prompt for those who new to the practice is to offer these two possibilities: "God, you are like a _____ (stone, GPS, alarm clock, starfish, cursor, measuring tape, bar of soap)" or "God, my life is like a _____ (piece of chalk, padlock, onion, pine cone)."

An IT litany

Giving thanks for the faith-oriented uses of Internet technology can be an understanding-expansion exercise for two groups. One group is composed of critics of technology. Another group includes those who use technology constantly in work but don't consider it a spiritual tool. A few examples to get going:

- I am thankful that Skype puts me in touch with my son who is deployed.

- I am thankful for my iPod when I need my own music to calm me down so I do not become angry.

- I am thankful for Freedom when I need to put distractions beyond my reach.

6

FAITH TIME IN THE AGE OF FACETIME

Social Media and the Church

One of the questions we asked ourselves when we started working on this book was: Why is it important for a church to be connected to the community through social media? How can the new technologies facilitate faith connections?

Sites like Facebook, Twitter, Instagram, LiveJournal, and Google+ have flourished as a way for people to connect in such mind-blowing ways that we have little to compare it to since the invention of the printing press! The choices for networking and making connections can be exhausting, so it makes sense that churches are hesitant to embrace using these tools. Should we use edited footage on YouTube to post about Vacation Bible School? Would an Advent Twitter feed reach people traveling this holiday season and keep them connected with their church family while abroad? Do people want a minister to post the complete text of sermons on the church site every week? How do we decide between what we want to share, what we should be doing to connect, and what should remain within the firmer boundaries of the faith family?

The fact that we have become so accessible can be intimidating, but it also means it's much easier for people with limited computer experience to excel at creating online communities. This means it's possible and important to try to learn about options available to reach all kinds of people—instead of only the ones who make it into the pews every week.

• ••• •

Daniel Ross-Jones struggles with these ideas every day, not only because his work is with youth and young adults (and he has to keep up or risk losing their interest), but because he too grew up with often conflicting circles of influence—the church and the worldwide web:

"To me, the answer to this question is the rhetorical, 'How can one feel it's unimportant for the church to stay connected using social media?' The church's mission, its core being of functioning as church, is entirely based in being together. Prioritizing different types of connection and relationship to the exclusion of others, that is to say, making a decision that door-to-door canvassing is better than creating an online forum and so abandoning an on-line presence entirely, siphons off time and resources that could otherwise be used to build up the community of Christ.

"As Protestants, our very tradition owes a debt of gratitude to capitalizing on the social media of the time five hundred or so years ago. Martin Luther's ability to capitalize on the Western development of the printing press and his conviction to use it to put scripture into the hands of the people, in their own language and style, sounds not dissimilar to the so-called democratization of media currently underway, fueled by emerging Internet technologies."

This ability to move forward, to face new challenges in reaching people yearning for a faith connection, is a critical aspect of our work in the church. In mainline Protestant communities, we tend to be especially wary of anything that reeks of evangelism, not because at its core it's a terrible thing, but because it is currently associated with much more conservative theological foundations. We are so afraid of being seen as pressuring people into the pews that we ignore the possibility that many people have no idea how different each church can be. These people may have had a bad experience with one church, or they may never have gone to church at all. Some might not even be looking for the more traditional brick and mortar experience but still feel a longing for a life of compassion, justice, and love.

When we sent out feelers for this book, we had a specific idea in mind. How could we begin to pray in a new, uncomfortable way that combined time we spent reading e-mail, texting, and updating friends about our lives in a limited number of characters, with intentional reflection that might bring us closer to God and our own community of faith. One of our contributors, Cody Maynus, took on this challenge with determination. He edited mercilessly to try to discover the significance of trimming a prayer to its essence and to its most intimate moment with God:

"It was nice to have the editorial directive to limit my prayers—address, attribute, supplication, closing—to 140 characters (the allowed limit of a tweet). The simplicity of the prayers was lovely and unexpected. I'm normally verbose when I write, especially if the writing is religious in nature. God, I think, is often kept in a nice, neat, little spiritual box in the sky. Our Christian faith, however, is an embodied one—one in which God became flesh and lived, ate, danced, fell in love, burped, and hung out with friends as a human being. Our prayers tend to reflect a God who is mystical and spiritual, not quite near enough to grasp and certainly not near enough to high five. Using such a common and generally secular (again, if the distinctions even exist) medium like Twitter to offer these simple and, I hope, heartfelt prayers strangely felt right."

Not many of us were able to create prayers as brief as his. We found ourselves cutting back and rewriting, but still we had trouble reaching the core of the prayer in this way. Why does it matter? To us, the desire to write this book emerged when we began to notice that people had stopped paying attention. We would be out to dinner with friends and if someone hadn't pulled out a phone within the first five minutes, it was a pleasant surprise. This happened everywhere, we noticed, and with people of every age and background. The attention span for even ordinary conversation had sunk so low. How could people handle more vulnerable, sacred discussion? Was anyone making time for it outside the church, and if so, what did that look like? Could the sacred be hiding inside those ordinary, distractible moments, just waiting for someone like Cody to make it succinct and available?

He wasn't the only one working to fit prayer into available formats. Sue Donnelly's prayers came from e-mails she wrote to a friend struggling with cancer. Although she couldn't be with this person through every chemo appointment or terrible morning, she found a way to affirm their friendship, love, and connection to the Holy Spirit in the simplest way available to her. When she reflected about that experience, she recognized that it was a small step toward discerning the most important connections that could be made through this medium:

"I've been thinking a lot about the ever-present battle with distractions. Facebook and e-mail and smart phones are tools to create connections—but much of the time they distract us from true exchanges and mutual understanding. I've been praying for myself how to not be a slave to it all, how to think about my days and experiences, friends and dreams, in more than status updates and funny texts. I pray that God will help me see ways to make real connections with the people I care about. I pray that I can attend to God in all the ways She is near despite the constant competing noise. This experience reinforced that there is something powerful about committing a prayer into words on paper or screen. The act of writing makes the words burn longer and louder. The written prayer resurfaces more freely throughout the day and serves as an interface between my hectic busyness and my yearning soul."

Does this sound scary? Or does it seem like these writers are doing something that already fits into our spiritual practices in a surprisingly familiar way? Opening the church up to social media doesn't mean throwing away the things we hold dear about our own experiences of prayer and connection. Doing so would be disingenuous. We aren't trying to tear anything apart; what we want to do is allow ourselves the opportunity to embrace sacred reflection.

When we were talking about this book a few months ago over e-mail (a technological blessing we rarely acknowledge given that it closes a 3,000-mile gap), we expressed some of the reasons we felt so deeply moved to share these ideas. We'll see if you can guess which one of us is which . . .

"I have been going to church regularly my whole life, and even though I'm familiar with the rituals, the prayers, the order of service, and the outreach, there are many times when I feel torn about my involvement. I'm often defensive about being a young Christian when I'm not in the embrace of my own church because that word—Christian—has gained some ugly baggage. I find myself having to explain, again and again, to friends who are appalled I would associate with "those people" that not every person who calls herself a Christian has a message of hate or intolerance.

"Whenever I have to do this, either in person or online, I feel that much lonelier in my faith. The Internet promises connection with like-minded people, but it's difficult to find a message to believe in amidst all the distractions. Are there blogs written by thoughtful, questioning, open people who are trying to live out faith in this strange new world of anonymous bullying and overly precious sound bites? Of course. Are there enough of them? I say no. Just as each of us has a responsibility to the health of the planet, to our loved ones, and to seeking true justice, we have a duty to share messages of tolerance, compassion, and support for all people beyond the pulpit." Who am I?

"I saw the face of a grandmother first glimpsing her granddaughter on Skype, and it was a blessing. I connected First Nations Canadian congregations with an Aotearoan White Ribbon Worship service, and even though it is a great sorrow that violence against women is experienced across the world, the trust between these two communities was a blessing. I became, really became, a young high-school-aged woman's pastor because I found and read the fanfic she had written on LiveJournal. (I even found old episodes of the show she wrote about online and watched them.) I carried beloved photographs to a memorial service on a flashdrive, and a very old gentleman pointed to it and said, 'That's a holy little jigger, isn't it?' I played a YouTube clip about the rescue of laboratory beagles at a Blessing of the Animals service. In Lent and Advent, I write prayers every day, and I put them on Facebook. Fixing my church's website is on my to-do list and it made my January resolutions for the third time! Everybody gets to laugh at me. That's a blessing.

"I am and will always be six steps behind the most current technological advances, which is wonderful for two reasons. First, I must keep walking—no resting on my links or laurels. Secondly, I learn and relearn how to trust others, really trust them with a shared ministry. I have to ask for help. They know I am not pretending! They can feel enfranchised and empowered in the church context. I love being behind but still on the path—it makes me feel like a disciple." Who am I?

Just look at all of the wonderful contributors who have written prayers and worship for this book. Because the Internet has made it easier for us to reach out to people around the world, we have been blessed with a rainbow of experiences to pray into. Our faith is made stronger and more resilient by connection with others, and as Daniel told us, "How a church facilitates faith conversations within a congregation is the best indicator of how it will do so with current and emerging media. This is a growth opportunity for most churches." This means that any healthy, dialoguing congregation can make use of social media if only they push themselves to explore something new.

• ● ● •

One challenge in using current technology to reach an audience marginalized or out of sync with the church is, how to we keep up? What's popular seems to change every month, and it's difficult to focus on modernizing the church without making current members feel unimportant. Daniel has an interesting perspective on this issue:

"I've received this question before as part of my work as communications director for a middle judicatory body. My answer is this: take a walk around any mainline Protestant church building constructed in the mid-twentieth century and open closet doors near classrooms and the sanctuary. Odds are pretty good these spaces will be filled with felt boards, filmstrips, and groovy wall banners.

"As the church, we've been caught in changing technology before. Even as the modern church, since the Industrial Revolution, we've changed technologies and methods. Sometimes that change has brought the newer tool alongside the older method, like hymn boards in sanctuaries while distributing typeset, duplicated worship folders to the faithful. Other times that change has supplanted the old, like moving from an old mimeograph machine to a photocopier.

"The key as a leader is to shepherd the congregation through this change as a sense of mission. Change for the sake of change is uninspiring, worthy of any backlash. Yet the church seals its own fate as an uninteresting relic of the past when it digs its heels deep and claims allegiance to a world that no longer exists. Such positions are neither missional nor Christian."

To this we say, Amen! Ministers don't write the same sermon year to year, do they? Parishioners are not expected to take one position in faith and hold to it like a stubborn pup for their entire lives, right? No! As parts of the body of Christ, we are challenged to argue, to learn, to observe, and, most importantly, to be open. When Jesus healed a man who could neither speak nor hear in chapter 7 of Mark, he did not say to him "Listen!" or "Speak!" but, rather, "Ephphatha—Be opened." Is this the easiest part of our faith? Definitely not. Even those of us who are proud of how tolerant and progressive we are (and oh yes, are we ever proud of this!) often fall short when it comes to uprooting traditions we hold dear.

It's so comfortable to do things the way we've always done them. Each of us loves certain hymns, a particular type of sermon—even the smell in the sanctuary may be precious and familiar. That being said, as a people of faith, we are desperately needed in the modern world. Our willingness to pray for strangers, to take on tasks that others shun, to be a safe haven for the battered and weary? Those are crucial, beautiful parts of doing Christ's work, and whether it's posting a compassionate tweet today or trying to understand the technologies of tomorrow, it is our duty to work at just these things we don't understand so that we can offer our gifts to others in a format that is comfortable and familiar to them.

So where do we begin? How do we decide the best approach for our church, our community, our staff? Every community of faith is different, of course, so there's no way to answer those questions conclusively. On top of that, as anyone who has been poking around the Internet for a while knows, some sites are thriving while others have become relics—as useless to us as filmstrips or carbon copies—so when the decision is made to reach out, it's important to do a little research first.

The best advice we can offer is this: Ask questions, then be prepared to listen. In other words, be opened. The congregation, children, friends, colleagues from seminary, and those new folks met at annual meeting—they are all fantastic resources, especially if the staff of the church doesn't happen to know a blog post from an instant message! For a minister, it can be especially difficult to pause and allow for others' guidance. It is even harder if the path leads away from what has always been done. This brings us to another point: if there is a commitment to exploring faith in this potentially unfamiliar and uncomfortable new landscape, the church, its members, and its minister must be willing to humble themselves to prepare for the journey together.

While these initial stages are difficult, once it's clear how people in the community communicate with each other on a daily basis, this outreach will have a place to begin. Perhaps a church will start small and work on keeping its website up to date. This seems menial, but many a congregation has been passed over by seekers who can't glean information online. Young people especially are used to being completely informed before making a decision about whether an event or group is worth their time, but everyday more professionals, working parents, and those dependent on carpooling look to church websites to decide what's a good fit. If a site is out of date or hard to use, potential congregants may presume the same is true of the community; the church risks having others judge and dismiss it as being out of touch. There won't be a chance to wow people with the message of the sermons or innovative after-worship forums if nobody new walks through the door.

Maybe the church has already knocked it out of the park with the website (while working on this project, we have seen the good, the bad, and the ugly, and the good has made us wish we could travel across the country to try out a church based solely on what was seen), and it feels ready to do more with what's freely available online. This is where we would ideally love to see every church, at a minimum—prepared, accessible, and excited to push faith into a new focus. This is where all the research can be put into action.

Does the church have a thriving youth group that might benefit from using Picasa, Flickr, or YouTube to share their projects with the wider community? Or could those same savvy kids help out by starting their own Facebook page as an offshoot of the church's, where they might set up weekly or monthly lunch meet-ups so that the camaraderie they share during youth group can be carried over to parts of their lives that are more stressful? Does that desire to stay connected have to be limited to the youth? Is there a men's breakfast group? A Bible study? A particularly busy committee? Plenty of sites have simple ways for these people to interact with each other, to plan, and to get excited about the life of the church.

In a profession that already demands the extra mile so often, many pastors are content to let this part of the job pass them by, or at the very least don't appreciate the opportunities it can provide. "I don't know what ministry will look like in the next year, ten years, fifty years," Cody says, "but I think that social media gives faith communities the unique opportunity to respond to a deep spiritual hunger that is not being satisfied by the traditional parish structure."

How, then, can churches allow themselves to pass by people who are hungering for God's word? It's part of a minister's genetic code to connect with people, to go tell it on the mountain . . . the mountain just looks a little different these days. It requires new tools to climb—the great news is, we don't have to do this alone. Did you notice how we got the congregation involved in the social media they want before even suggesting that the staff commit to much more than a website upgrade? That's because a minister's job is a little different when it comes to this kind of outreach; it's not enough for a spiritual leader to use these tools without preparation. What we need more of when it comes to the church extending itself outside of its comfortable walls is reflection, not clichéd sentimental sound bites. Using these new tools thoughtfully may be a task a minister approaches on his or her own, or it may be a community effort (even better would be some combination of both), and it will look wildly different in every faith family.

Some pastors might like to start off with something as simple as Formspring, a website that creates virtual office hours when people may come, anonymously or not, and ask in a public forum any question they may have. In other churches, groups may form around the idea of a Lenten reflection, or the study of a particular text, and those people may be inspired to write and share their discussions with the larger community. This is where a church can get creative. Is it a visual or tech savvy congregation? Record those discussions and put them online for others to see and comment on. Maybe the group prefers a more traditional template, like a blog, where one or more members can post meditations. It doesn't matter what is chosen, as long as people are willing to explore the options to find something that truly opens the relationship with God. Remember that while the process of choosing a format is important, it shouldn't obscure the larger picture—the point of this is to share in a discussion about the holy we find in ordinary moments, and more importantly, in ourselves.

• • •

We asked our contributors whether it is possible to take what is essentially an advertising tool (social media as evangelism) and turn it into something that can truly serve people, whether they come to church or not, on a spiritual level?

The difficulty with reaching out to people using the tools we're most familiar with in this moment is that they've already been relegated to a few basic uses. We get and send e-mails with adorable pictures accompanied by Bible quotes; Facebook is filled with the same sort of thing, with the added bonus of the "like" button popularity contest. Other sites, like Twitter or Tumblr, tend to stay out of the religious arena as much as possible because the firestorms incited by a misunderstood post are so filled with vitriol that they completely obscure the point of the original message.

In the church, though, discussion is often the point. The major difference is that when standing face to face, it can be much more difficult to say the sorts of things people freely type online. Real anger and hurt may be expressed in both forums, but when dealing with new media, an expectation of mutual respect must be a part of the program. (It goes without saying that this is also true within the physical church community!) It is possible to create this kind of safe space on many forums, but research will be necessary. We can't predict what will work for a faith community today or five or fifty years from now, but fortunately, plenty of people within the church are passionate about expanding the conversation beyond the walls of the congregation, and they will always be the best resource for current trends.

One of the most important things ministers in particular can do to encourage respectful dialogue is to preach about social media and Internet use often, lifting up with even hands the blessings and curses. Whether it's used by the church or not, the Internet exists, and it's a significant part of people's lives. Even the kindest people have been known to get swept up by a difference of opinion in that less accountable world, and most of us are, admittedly, only averagely compassionate. This means we're probably guilty of using social media to brag, challenge, or demean others in some way. It's easy to think of the words we type as fleeting and unimportant, but the potential for bullying, and the lasting effects of it, are devastating. This is not limited to teenage drama either; cruelty exists far past puberty, and we all need reminders about the importance of good conduct. Even a church whose preacher never prays in 140 characters should take part in this larger conversation!

When we talked to Cody about his interest in blending the lines of faith and the secular world, he said, "God has always used the normal, ordinary, 'nonholy' elements to represent or, in fact, embody the divine. I think immediately of bread and wine. There's nothing inherently holy about bread and wine. When the church uses these elements, however, something truly remarkable happens and Christ is made present for the worshiping community.

"Even though humankind was made in the likeness and image of God, the difference between human and divine is generally apparent. Yet it was humankind through which God chose to manifest God's self in the person of Jesus Christ—something not holy is made the pinnacle of holiness. If bread and wine can become Christ and a little child born in a cow stall can become God, why can't Twitter become evangelism?"

Evangelism is the sharing of the good news.

This is so deeply true, and yet it is often forgotten in our struggle to get through the week between benediction and prelude. God is everywhere. God is for all people. Never place a period where God has placed a comma. We say these words, but can we really commit to living them out? Can we seek out God in the ordinary, the uncomfortable, the ever changing? Can we enter the places where we don't see God immediately and trust our faith to guide us into much needed community?

The common people of the digital age include Tumblr teenagers, people experiencing debilitating mental or physical illness whose window on the world is Facebook, immigrants clicking translation sites, the underemployed or overworked at library monitors—the list goes on and on. They are searching for a faith family that looks squarely at their truths without smoothing over the rough edges. They may be hoping for acceptance. Others may search for a place where a part of them that has been made to seem shameful will be embraced, examined, or healed. All want to know that their concerns are a part of the gathered community.

We will discover, together, the ways worship can be relevant to the world we live in and all of God's seeking hopeful children. This is our ministry as evolving people embracing that slippery thing called faith.

Contributors

• • •

Vince Amlin, 11, 34, 38, 80–81, 168

Lina Andronoviene, 67, 75, 141–42

Elizabeth D. Barnum, 34, 41, 60, 62, 76

Molly Phinney Baskette, 4, 40, 41, 42–43, 68, 164

Sharon A. Benton, 2, 44, 55, 70–72, 86, 87–88, 93–95, 97–98, 104, 107, 113, 114, 125–26, 129, 131, 154

Elaine E. Bolitho, 136–37, 142

Richard Bott, 16, 36–37, 44–45, 64, 90–91, 115

Matthew Braddock, 31, 54–55, 60–61, 153

Barbara Bruce Brakey, 23–24, 78–79

Diane Lamoureux Ciba, 49

Devoree Clifton Crist, 44, 69, 71–75, 95–96, 104, 113–14, 141, 159, 163, 165, 173

John H. Danner, 87, 100, 108, 117, 125, 127

Isobel de Gruchy, ix, 47, 53–54, 57, 58

Sue B. Donnelly, 3–4, 13, 45–46, 73–74, 78, 181–82

LL Kroouze DuBreuil, 12, 48, 55, 92–93, 111, 118, 136

Erice C. Fairbrother, 17, 18–19, 21–22, 25, 29, 50–51, 64–65, 132–34

Katie Fiegenbaum (translator), 13, 52–53, 123–24

Lynne Frith, 35–36, 40–41, 43, 56–57, 59, 67, 69

Kipp Gilmore-Clough, 15–16, 18, 19, 44, 83–84, 113, 135–36

Carol Hallman, 68

Mary Beth Hartenstein, 39, 58, 77, 79, 109, 151

Abigail Hastings, 87, 101–2

Jerry Hebenstreit, 12, 31, 50, 62, 69, 71, 72, 82, 85, 86, 89–90, 99, 105, 122, 126, 127–28, 130–31, 160, 162

Cheri R. Holdridge, 32–33, 138–39, 151–53

Index of Topics

• • •

Other Pilgrim Press books from Maren Tirabassi and Maria Mankin

ALL WHOM GOD HAS JOINED
Resources for Clergy and Same-Gender Loving Couples
LEANN MCCALL TIGERT AND MAREN C. TIRABASSI
Paperback/$20.00

This book is a unique collection of liturgical and ceremonial resources as well as pastoral care tools and insights on same-sex covenanting ceremonies. It is designed for clergy and couples addressing these issues.

BEFORE THE AMEN
Creative Resources for Worship
MAREN C. TIRABASSI AND MARIA I. TIRABASSI
Paperback/$20.00

Before the Amen is a worship anthology that evolved from the bestselling title *Touch Holiness: Resources for Worship* (The Pilgrim Press, 1990). The Tirabassis provide fresh language inclusive of gender, ethnicity, race, age, orientation, and ability. Nine chapters of seasonal materials, three chapters of sacraments and services, and seven chapters oriented by topic are provided with a host of other useful information.

CARING FOR OURSELVES
While Caring for Our Elders
MAREN C. TIRABASSI, MARIA I. TIRABASSI AND LEANNE MCCALL TIGERT
Paperback/$16.00

Caring for Ourselves: While Caring for Our Elders shares the true stories of family members who are caring for elderly loved ones. *Caring for Ourselves: While Caring for Our Elders* gives an overview of some of the psychological issues involved in contemporary elder care, and the second chapter approaches some overarching biblical themes. Following these introductory sections are twenty-five brief yet edifying chapters that tell the stories of some remarkably honest people who are caring for elderly loved ones.

DAYBOOK FOR NEW VOICES
A Calendar of Reflections and Prayers by and for Youth
MAREN C. TIRABASSI AND MARIA I. TIRABASSI, CO-EDITORS
Paperback/$18.00

DayBook for New Voices: A Calendar of Reflections and Prayers by and for Youth is a collection of prayers, poems, and reflections for every day of the year, written primarily by youth. It is a follow-up book to Maren C. Tirabassi's popular *Blessing New Voices: Prayers of Young People and Worship Resources for Youth Ministry* (2000).

GIFTS IN OPEN HANDS
More Worship Ideas for the Global Community
MAREN TIRABASSI AND KATHY WONSON EDDY
Paperback/$28.00

Gifts in Open Hands: More Worship Ideas for the Global Community was inspired by the bestselling *Gifts of Many Cultures: Worship Resources for the Global Community*, also by Maren Tirabassi and Kathy Wonson Eddy (1995, United Church Press). *Gifts in Open Hands* contains multicultural liturgies, prayers, affirmations, blessings, and poetry by people from the global community. Black-and-white images for reproduction in church bulletins is included, and a new feature is the arrangement of translations so that materials in other languages are available to English-speaking as well as bilingual worship planners. There are also additional graphics and musical resources.

GIFTS OF MANY CULTURES
Worship Resources for the Global Community
MAREN C. TIRABASSI AND KATHY WONSON EDDY
Paperback/$28.00

A moving collection of liturgical resources from the global community, *Gifts of Many Cultures* will enrich the worship life of congregations in all denominations. Tirabassi and Eddy have developed an anthology of original prayers, poetry, stories, and readings for: sermons; invocations; calls to worship; confessions; liturgies for Holy Communion and baptism; guided meditations, songs, and drawings; and other resources designed around the seasons of the church year.

To order these or any other books from The Pilgrim Press call or write to:

THE PILGRIM PRESS
700 PROSPECT AVENUE EAST
CLEVELAND, OHIO 44115-1100

PHONE ORDERS: 1-800-537-3394   ■   FAX ORDERS: 216-736-2206
Please include shipping charges of $6.00 for the first book and
$0.75 for each additional book.
Or order from our web sites at www.pilgrimpress.com and www.ucpress.com.

Prices subject to change without notice.